29. 50

# CHARITABLE GIVING AND TAX-EXEMPT ORGANIZATIONS

## The Impact of the 1981 Tax Act

# Other Ronald Press
# Books by the Author

The Law of Tax-Exempt
Organizations (3rd ed. 1979)

The Law of Tax-Exempt
Organizations, 1980 Supplement

The Law of Tax-Exempt
Organizations, 1981 Supplement

Charity Under Siege:
Government Regulation of
Fund Raising (1980)

# BRUCE R. HOPKINS

*Member of the*
*District of Columbia Bar*

# CHARITABLE GIVING AND TAX-EXEMPT ORGANIZATIONS

The Impact of the 1981 Tax Act

A RONALD PRESS
PUBLICATION

JOHN WILEY & SONS
New York · Chichester
Brisbane · Toronto · Singapore

ISBN 0-471-86736-5

Printed in the United States of America

10 9 8 7 6 5 4 3 2 1

To my parents,

Jane D. and Frederick B. Hopkins

# Preface

The newly enacted Economic Recovery Tax Act of 1981 is an extraordinary law, even as federal tax measures go. From general reading as the act evolved, one was able to come to understand its broad outlines and ultimately its general contents when it was, at the end, rushed to enactment. But, the final product actually in hand, its nearly 200 pages can be plumbed for hours, as amendment after amendment offers up tantalizing opportunity for tax planning and new questions out of newly provided answers.

Probably the Act touches every individual, business and other entity, and cuts across all fields of law. However, the new law has particular consequences for one sector of society on which it originally was to have little if any effect: the nation's nonprofit sector, certainly the charitable organizations and institutions in that group. The purpose of this book is to explain these consequences of the provisions of the Act affecting nonprofit groups and the tax treatment of contributions to them.

The Act was introduced in the House of Representatives as H.R. 4242. It was reported by the House Committee on Ways and Means on July 24, 1981 (H. Rep. No. 97-201) and passed on House on July 29, 1981. Meanwhile, the Senate Committee on Finance was using a previous House-passed measure (H. J. Res. 266) as a vehicle for tax revisions and reported a tax proposal on July 6, 1981 (S. Rep. No. 97-144). This proposal was considered throughout July and passed the Senate on July 31 as its version of H. R. 4242. The two measures were reconciled in conference, with the Senate agreeing to the conference report (S. Rep. No. 97-176) on August 3, 1981, and the House agreeing to the conference report (H. Rep. No. 97-215) on August 4, 1981. The measure was signed into law by President

Ronald Reagan on August 13, 1981, as Public Law 97-34 (95 Stat. 172).

Throughout the book, references to the Economic Recovery Tax Act of 1981 are to the "Act" and references to the Internal Revenue Code of 1954, as amended, are to the "Code."

BRUCE R. HOPKINS

*Washington, D.C.*
*November 1981*

# CONTENTS

# CHARITABLE GIVING AND TAX-EXEMPT ORGANIZATIONS

## The Impact of the 1981 Tax Act

# 1

# The 1981 Tax Act in Perspective

In recent years, tax revision and charitable giving have not mixed very well. While the basic charitable contribution deductions (income, estate and gift) have been part of federal tax law since its inception, and thus have long been taken for granted by donors and their charitable donees, past years have witnessed a variety of erosions in the tax incentive for charitable giving. For many taxpayers, *a* charitable contribution deduction is not enough; only the *maximum* charitable deduction will now suffice.

The Tax Reform Act of 1969 brought a wholesale rewriting of the federal tax laws relating to charitable giving and the tax treatment of charitable organizations themselves. In many ways, the 1969 Act greatly increased the tax incentives for charitable giving (although it imposed rigorous law on some nonprofit organizations). However, with only a few exceptions, the tax support for charitable giving has been on the decline ever since.

The reason for this decline is simple: The contemporary definition of "tax reform" has been "tax simplification." Tax simplification looks to streamline and shorten tax laws and forms. Antithetical to tax simplification and reform are new tax deductions, credits, exclusions, exemptions, and other "preferences".[1] Thus, proposals such as a charitable deduction for nonitemizers were opposed by some tax planners because it would add lines to the tax forms.

Another dimension to tax simplification is to expand the use of certain tax law features to make income tax return preparation easier. Prominent of these features is the standard deduction (now the "zero bracket amount"), for its users are generally

---

[1]For a complex nation, the term tax "simplification" can be an oversimplification. The true objective should be tax "equity," which, to be achieved, requires some exceptions or stimuli here and there throughout the tax system. While some tax revisions get fairly or unfairly tagged as plums for "special interests," most are legitimate revisions of law designed to further social policy. Thus, a fair tax structure for a complex political, social, and economic system should itself be, and not surprisingly, "complex."

For example, the guiding spirit principally permeating the development of the Carter Administration's tax proposals was the ephemeral concept of simplicity. In June 1977, then Treasury Secretary W. Michael Blumenthal stated that the Carter Administration's "goals are to make the American tax system simpler, fairer and better able to foster growth and efficiency in the American economy." And in September 1977, Secretary Blumenthal remarked that the federal tax "system is far too complex." However, three weeks later, President Carter observed that "tax reform . . . is, as I have discovered recently, an extremely complicated matter."

The perils of over-pursuit of tax simplification were nicely articulated in a tax simplification study by the staff of the Joint Committee on Taxation published on September 19, 1977. The essence of this analysis is that there are competing, legitimate tax policy goals, such as equity, efficiency, and economic and social objectives, which necessarily and unavoidably contribute to tax complexity. The staff observed that "often, the reconciliation of competing principles or objectives results in the introduction of complexity and intricate detail into the tax system" and that "the crux of the issue, then, is the degree of complication acceptable in exchange for the increased realization of other valued goals." Thus, while the elimination of itemized deductions would theoretically simplify the tax laws and broaden the income tax base, the staff recognized the basic fact that the charitable deduction "serves as an incentive for charitable giving."

saved the toils of records retention and deductions calculation. However, the greater the use of the standard deduction the lesser the use of the itemized deductions, with the consequence that this tax reform eroded the utility of the specific deductions, including the charitable contribution deduction.

The third relevant dimension to tax simplification is that it can easily lead to calls for tax reduction, on the theory that elimination or minimization of tax preferences broadens the tax base and thus facilitates across-the-board tax rate cuts. While tax slashes are always politically popular and sometimes economically warranted, they unfortunately reduce the value of all deductions, including the charitable contribution deduction.

Thus, tax legislation since 1969, although containing some provisions specifically benefiting charitable giving, has done much to erode it. Tax rates (on income, estates, and capital gain) have been lowered, the standard deduction increased, and ways of transferring property for tax benefit (other than by charitable gift) have been created. Few if any of these changes have been implemented to deliberately penalize philanthropy. Rather, the adverse repercussions are a by-product of the formulation of other tax policy—although nonetheless just as real.

The Economic Recovery Tax Act of 1981 carries on this pattern. The purpose of the Act is to encourage economic growth in the United States, and to this end the law created by the Act reduces individual and corporate tax rates, introduces new incentives for savings, and eases much of the estate and gift tax liability.

As discussed in Chapter 2, the Act contains some provisions of direct benefit to philanthropy, most notably a charitable contribution deduction for individuals who do not otherwise itemize deductions and an increase in the charitable deduction allowable to corporations. But, as discussed in Chapter 4, this progress is more than offset by the new rules that will adversely affect tax-motivated charitable giving.

There are several reasons for this:

- The true economic worth of any tax deduction is measurable only in relation to the tax rate against which it is applied. A deduction is worth more in juxtaposition to high rates and less as the rates come down. The charitable contribution deduction is not immune from this tax rule. The Act lowers tax rates (income, estate and gift) and the value of the charitable deduction will suffer accordingly.

- Many charitable organizations rely heavily on gifts of property for their support. One of the tax incentives for a donor that induces the parting with the property is the avoidance of the tax on the capital gain that would occur if the property was otherwise transferred. This incentive is lessened to the extent the capital gain tax rates are reduced, and the Act is causing just that.

- Tax-motivated charitable giving competes with other ways to transfer money or property for tax advantage. The difficulty for charity in this regard is compounded to the extent that the alternative modes of transfer can be done so that the transferor receives, in addition to tax benefit for the transaction, ultimate return of the principal transferred and favorable tax treatment of the earnings thereon. To the detriment of charitable giving, the Act increases the utility of individual retirement accounts, and creates new ways for taxpayers to invest funds in return for tax-free interest.

- A considerable portion of charitable giving is done through estates. However, as estate tax rates are reduced, transfers to spouses are encouraged, and special low-valuation rules are expanded, the value of the estate (and to somewhat comparable degrees the gift) tax charitable contribution deduction is diminished. The Act causes all of this.

- Some transfers to charity that are predicated on tax incentives result when the donors have no real option, in that any other form of transfer is not palatable in terms of tax consequences (such as capital gain taxation). To the extent that the tax laws make it easier for a taxpayer to retain property, or to transfer it other than by charitable gift, the tax motivation for charitable giving is retarded. The Act does this along several tax fronts, such as by expanding the annual per donee gift tax exclusion, decreasing the necessity of the selling of family farms and closely held businesses to pay estate taxes, increasing the capital gain exclusion with respect to the sale of personal residences, and increasing the capital-gain-deferring rollover period following the sale of personal residences.

Again, it cannot be overemphasized that these tax changes are entirely meritorious and were propounded for reasons that have nothing to do with charitable giving. At the same time, the consequences for charitable giving of these changes are serious —and adverse.

The adverse impact on charitable giving to be caused by the Act was rarely reflected upon as the measure wended its way to enactment. However, soon thereafter, the consequences became all too apparent. For example, two weeks after the Act was signed into law, Independent Sector announced an analysis showing that over the next four years (1981–1984) the Act will trigger a loss to charitable organizations of $18.3 billion. Brian O'Connell, the organization's president, said that "this unintended side effect of the broader tax bill could weaken many of the very voluntary organizations the President and the public are counting on to make up for the federal budget cutbacks." If future giving habits continue to be influenced by tax considerations, O'Connell added, "giving is certain to decline, but to the extent we can stimulate the other larger motivations for giving, we can begin to solve the problem and strengthen the basic fiber of the country." He concluded that "just to stay even, and certainly to fulfill increased expectations for expanded service, we are going to have to convince people to significantly increase their levels of giving."[2]

The study upon which the Independent Sector announcement was based was written at The Urban Institute.[3] This study attributed the losses to the individual tax rate reductions (thereby increasing the "price of giving") on income (both the regular and maximum tax) and capital gain. (The estimated loss

[2]The quotations are from an Independent Sector news release dated August 27, 1981.

[3]Clotfelter and Salamon, "The Federal Government and the Nonprofit Sector; The Impact of the 1981 Tax Act on Individual Charitable Giving" (The Urban Institute, August 1981).

does not include any losses potentially forthcoming as the result of revisions in the estate, gift and corporate tax rules, or the indexing and many other provisions.) Matters may be even more serious for the charitable community in that the $18.3 billion is an estimated net reduction, reflecting increased giving by reason of the coming increase in discretionary income, general growth in overall income stimulated by the Reagan Administration's economic program, and additional giving stimulated by the new charitable contribution deduction for individuals who do not otherwise itemize deductions.[4] One of the study's authors echoed the concerns of Independent Sector, saying that "the impacts of the tax legislation are all the more significant coming as they do on top of the pressure that will be put on nonprofit organizations as a consequence of the other half of the Economic Recovery Program: federal budget cuts."[5]

Projected over the four-year period, the gift losses are as follows: $0.5 billion in 1981, $3.3 billion in 1982, $5.5 billion in 1983, and $9 billion in 1984. The study is properly quick to note that individual giving to charity is expected to increase by about 14 percent through the period ending in 1984, and thus that the projected decline in giving attributable to the Act is relative to what would have occurred under prior law (and therefore is not a decline in absolute terms). The belief, then, is that the Act will severely stunt the growth of charitable giving rather than prevent any growth at all.

The study raises two additional points. First, an effect of the Act in the charitable giving context is that the decline in contributions by individuals will not occur equally up and down the tax brackets. Foreseen from 1981 to 1984 is a 12 percent decline in giving by taxpayers at the high economic levels (the top 15 percent), a modest increase of 2 percent in giving by taxpayers at the low economic levels (the bottom 30 percent) and a considerable increase (11 percent) in giving by taxpayers in the middle economic levels (the remaining 55 percent). These

[4]See Chapter 2 § 2.
[5]Remarks of Lester M. Salamon, in Independent Sector news release, *supra* n. 2.

variations are attributed by the study to the fact that the Act "delivers considerably more tax advantages to upper-income taxpayers than to middle-or lower-income taxpayers," and consequently removes some of the tax advantages of the charitable contributions deductions (and does so at the very levels where the deduction is worth the most).

Second, the study predicts a shift in the types of exempt activities and organizations that will receive the real increase in individual giving projected for the 1981–1984 period. The prospects are for religious organizations to receive 76 percent of the increase in individual giving during this period (a 17.4 percent increase), contrasted with a decline in individual giving to educational institutions and hospitals by over 3 percent. The reason for this phenomenon is closely tied to the reason for the previous point: "Generally speaking, lower-income groups give proportionately more of their charitable gifts to religious organizations than do the rich, while the rich give proportionately more to educational and cultural institutions."[6] Once again, the Act's tax advantages will work to partially undermine the charitable deduction by eroding the tax incentive to give to charity, particularly among the more affluent donors, and thus result in a variation in the extent of support flowing to the categories of charitable recipients.

The Urban Institute study concludes that "[i]t should be clear from the evidence presented here that nonprofit organizations can anticipate a period of considerable strain as a consequence of the budget and tax policy changes recently adopted by the federal government." The analysis that follows bears out that conclusion. However, it is the author's sincere hope that an outcome of the experience of "considerable strain" will be an independent sector that receives amply more financial support than it would have otherwise and functions more productively and efficiently, and does so in an environment of supportive law and understanding regulators.

[6]This is the same type of outcome forecast by those contemplating a change from a federal income tax charitable contribution deduction to a charitable contribution credit.

There are those who, quite properly, are quick to point out that tax incentives are not the only reason persons contribute to charity and that the philanthropic community should not drastically alter present fund-raising programs until the effects of the Act are better known. For example, an analysis of the Act prepared by the American Association of Fund-Raising Counsel, Inc., concludes that "while the tax incentive for giving by wealthy individuals is a factor that at times determines the size of a gift, charitable organizations should not put less emphasis on large givers in favor of shifting to lower or middle income wage earners." The Urban Institute study was said to "prove that the nation's charitable organizations must be more professional and energetic in seeking private sources of funding." The AAFRC president, John J. Schwartz, added that these organizations "must give fund raising the highest priority and tailor programs to meet real proven needs." This analysis quotes a "veteran professional fund raising counselor" as stating that The Urban Institute study "sounds like a self-fulfilling prophecy" but that "the American people will never let it happen."[7]

In the three chapters to follow, a review is provided of the provisions of the Act as they relate to charitable giving and nonprofit organizations. Thereafter, in the concluding chapter, a brief look in these regards beyond the Act is taken.

[7]The quotations are from the AAFCR Giving USA Bulletin No. 7 (1981).

# 2

# The New Charitable Giving Rules

## § 2.1  Introduction

A superficial review of the elements of the Act likely leads the reviewer to believe that the Act is a bonanza for America's charities. (As discussed in Chapter 4, however, a closer examination of the Act finds a variety of provisions that will operate to erode the benefits of the charitable contributions deductions for federal income, gift and estate taxes.)

The Act contains two revisions of federal tax law that will have a direct, substantial, and favorable impact on the nation's charitable, educational, religious, scientific, health and like agencies and institutions: the creation of a charitable contribution deduction for individuals who do not (otherwise) itemize their deductions (§ 2 hereof) and an expansion of the charitable contribution deduction allowable to corporations (§ 3).

Other tax incentives for charitable organizations provided by the Act include a charitable contribution deduction for gifts of newly manufactured equipment to colleges and universities for research (§ 4), an estate and gift tax charitable contribution deduction for copyrightable works of art (§ 5), qualification of income interests created by charitable remainder trusts for the new unlimited marital deduction (§ 6), an investment tax credit for the rehabilitation of historic structures (§ 7), and revision of the rules concerning certain transfers of real property for conservation purposes (§ 8).

## § 2.2    Charitable Contribution Deduction for Individual Nonitemizers

(a)    Summary of Law Revision

Individuals who do not itemize their income tax deductions may nonetheless deduct charitable contributions, subject to certain limitations (Act § 121).

(b)    Effective Date

This law change becomes effective for tax years beginning after December 31, 1981.

(c)    Prior Law

The law antedating this revision did not allow the deductibility of charitable contributions by donors who do not itemize their deductions.

(d)    Reason for Revision

By reason of previous "tax reform" acts, the former standard deduction (now the "zero bracket amount") has been incrementally increased, in the process shrinking the base of the taxpayers who itemize their deductions and thus those who have a tax motivation for giving. Many feared this ongoing development was giving the charitable deduction the appearance of being a "tax loophole for the very wealthy."

The taxpayer who utilizes the standard deduction—which is now the case for about 75 percent of Americans—is precluded from using the charitable contribution deduction. In recent years, deliberate efforts have been made to attract taxpayers away from the task of itemizing deductions by increasing the standard deduction. The Tax Reform Act of 1976 alone shifted 5 percent of the taxpaying public into the ranks of the nonitemizers. The expansion of the reach of the standard deduction has been estimated to have chopped charitable giving by $5 billion since 1970. (During congressional hearings on the Carter Administration's tax package, representatives of the charitable sector testified that the proposed increase in the standard deduction would cause 7.7 million taxpayers to stop itemizing deductions and a resulting annual loss in contributions to charity of approximately $700 million.)

This expansion of the utility of the charitable deduction is intended to stimulate charitable giving and voluntarism and pump additional billions of dollars into the American nonprofit sector, thereby increasing the range and extent of the thousands of services and programs supported by the nation's nonprofit organizations.

(e)  Specifics of Law Revision

Due to an extraordinary amount of effort by the nation's philanthropic community spearheaded by a new organization named "Independent Sector," the above-the-line charitable contribution deduction became a reality when the Act was signed into law.

This new deduction, as finally enacted, reflects the political and economic realities that overshadowed its consideration. Two features of the measure were grudgingly accepted by the independent sector as conditions for its enactment: a phase-in of the extent of the deduction (which first takes effect for 1982) and a "sunsetting" of the rules (which are set to expire after 1986). By accepting these compromises, the independent sector headed off one of the principal goals of the Department of the Treasury, which was establishment of a "floor" consisting of an amount only above which contributions would be deductible,[1] and defused the greatest concern of the Treasury Department, which was (and is) the revenue loss associated with the expanded deduction.[2]

As a result, the charitable deduction for nonitemizers (Code

[1] A principal concern within the philanthropic community was that enactment of a "floor" under the charitable deduction (as is the case with the medical deduction) for nonitemizers would inevitably lead to a floor under the deduction for itemizers—a dreaded possibility.

[2] These "revenue losses" are estimated to be $33 million for fiscal year 1982, $280 million for fiscal year 1983, $390 million for fiscal year 1984, $1.291 billion in fiscal year 1985, and $2.827 billion in fiscal year 1986.

§ 170(i)) is now written so that (1) in 1982 and 1983, a donor can deduct 25 percent of the first $100 contributed to charity (thus, a maximum deduction of $25), (2) in 1984, a donor can deduct 25 percent of the first $300 contributed to charity (a maximum deduction of $75), (3) in 1985, a donor can deduct 50 percent of all contributions, and (4) in 1986, a donor can deduct all charitable contributions without otherwise itemizing deductions. However, the extent of allowability of any charitable deduction is governed by certain overall percentage limitations.[3]

The principal rationale for the above-the-line charitable deduction is that support for the nation's charitable sector is a matter of fundamental policy and philosophy underlying the very nature of the American system of government, which should give free play to private initiative and voluntarism. From this standpoint, the new deduction is not revolutionary tax legislation but merely tax policy being shaped in light of overall governmental policy and structure. This view was stated on the floor of the Senate during that body's consideration of the charitable contributions legislation by one of its principal proponents, Senator Daniel P. Moynihan (D-N.Y.), as follows:

> It [the new legislation] would . . . restore a bit more independence and vitality to the voluntary sector. It will add a bit to the ability of the ordinary working men and women to determine how, and on what, some of his or her money is spent. It will in some small measure retard the process that has been described as the slow but steady conquest of the private sector by the public.

> Accompanying a mounting wariness toward Government monopoly, there is a widening appreciation by the American people of the unique and vital role played by private, nonprofit organizations in our Nation's economy.

[3]In general, contributions in cash to public charities are deductible to the extent of 50 percent of the donor's adjusted gross income, contributions of property that has appreciated in value to public charities are deductible to the extent of 30 percent of the donor's adjusted gross income, and contributions to private foundations are deductible to the extent of 20 percent of the donor's adjusted gross income (Code § 170(b)(1)).

This appreciation predates the present administration. It constitutes the fundamental rationale for this legislation, which we first introduced in the 95th Congress. Moreover, it is familiar to every American as the basic principle of federalism: That the National Government should assume only those responsibilities that cannot satisfactorily be carried out by the States, by the localities, and by the myriad private structures and organizations, both formal and informal, that comprise the American society; structures that include the family itself, the neighborhood, the church, and the many private nonprofit agencies found in every community in this land.

\* \* \*

While I am in the Senate, this legislation will not be undone. For it will be shown to be among the most significant social policy advances of recent years. It will reinforce the fiscal underpinnings of the tens of thousands of voluntary organizations that embody this society's devotion to community, its dedication to common provision, and its predilection for what [de] Tocqueville called association. It will enhance one of mankind's noblest impulses: to give voluntarily of one's own earnings so that the lives of others will be better. It will retard the tendency to rely solely on Government to meet the needs of individuals and communities.[4]

Another rationale advanced by advocates of the expanded charitable contribution deduction was somewhat the same as the more philosophic justification but was more straightforward: the portion of an individual's income that is given to charity should not be taxed. Still another contention advanced was that the various increases in the standard deduction (the "zero bracket amount") in recent years outpaced the equivalent level of itemized deductions, so that a consequence was a relative decline in the amount of charitable giving. Yet another rationale was that government's best interests lie in adoption of the provision, in that, in the words of its other principal sponsor, Senator Bob Packwood (R-Ore.), it provides a considerable "bang for the buck,"[5] since the expanded deduction embodies a multiplier effect; for example, one estimate has been that the availability of the expanded charitable deduction in 1975 would have resulted in increased gifts to charity of $3.8 billion with an attendant revenue loss to the government of $3.2 billion.

[4]127 Cong. Rec. S7962 (daily ed. July 20, 1981).
[5]*Ibid.* at S7960.

A further rationale for the charitable contributions legislation was advanced—one that is peculiar to the circumstances in which it was considered. Congressional consideration of the tax legislation (and hence the new charitable deduction) came shortly after passage of the Reagan administration's budget cuts, which, it has been estimated,[6] will cause a loss during fiscal years 1981 to 1984 of about $110.4 billion to charitable organizations. There has been much hope expressed in and out of Congress that the expanded deduction will inject funding into private sector programs to enable that sector to continue the provision of some of the social services that heretofore have been the responsibility of government. Although it is readily apparent that the independent sector cannot shoulder all of these financial commitments, the hope has been expressed that the expanded charitable deduction can help to nurture support for continuation of at least some of these services.

## § 2.3    Expanded Charitable Contribution Deduction for Corporations

(a)    Summary of Law Revision

Contributions to charitable organizations are deductible by a corporation up to 10 percent of the corporation's taxable income (Act § 263).

(b)    Effective Date

This law change becomes effective for tax years beginning after December 31, 1981.

(c)    Prior Law

In the law antedating this revision, in a tax year a corporation could deduct up to 5 percent of the corporation's taxable in-

---

[6]Salamon and Abramson, "The Federal Government and the Non-Profit Sector: Implications of the Reagan Budget Proposals" (The Urban Institute, May 1981), reproduced at 127 Cong. Rec. S7964 (daily ed. July 20, 1981).

come as a charitable contribution. For this purpose, "taxable income" of a corporation is computed without regard to the charitable deduction rules, a variety of "special deductions" for corporations, the net operating loss carryback rules, and any capital loss carrybacks (Code § 170(b)(2)). Any charitable contributions made by a corporation in a tax year in excess of the amount deductible in a contribution year are generally deductible in each of the five succeeding tax years in order of time (Code § 170(d)(2)).

(d)   Reasons for Revision

The Act has been perceived in many quarters as being highly beneficial to business corporations. Enactment of the Act came soon after enactment of a wide range of cutbacks in federal budget outlays for a variety of social programs. This juxtaposition of new laws and the perceived contrast in impact led proponents of the revision to urge an easing of the corporate charitable contribution deduction limitation, in the hope that corporations would share some of their newfound tax benefits with the less fortunate by passing more contributions on to the charitable sector. Aside from the validity of this belief, the fact is that few corporations came even close to making charitable contributions up to the 5 percent limitation.

The sponsor of this revision, Senator Edward M. Kennedy (D-Mass.), described the rationale for the proposal as follows:

At the present time, corporate contributions to charity average only about 1.2 percent of corporate income, so the revenue loss for the amendment is extremely small. The Joint Economic Committee has estimated it to be less than $50 million a year, perhaps much less than that.

But some corporations are at their limit, so it is appropriate to increase the limit now.

One of the administration's justifications for the current reductions in Federal spending is that in many areas involving social programs, it will be appropriate for the private sector and voluntary agencies to increase their own efforts to meet the need. In fact, corporations are now being deluged with requests for assistance from social agencies facing funding cutoffs.

It is clear that private agencies cannot make up the full loss of Federal aid. The Urban Institute estimates that over the period 1981–84, Federal funds for welfare, health, and environment, housing, food, and the arts will be cut by over $128 billion.

Voluntary agencies working in this area will suffer a direct loss of some $27 billion over the next 5 years, or about $5 billion a year.

Contributions to nonprofit groups by corporations and some 600 company-operated foundations totaled about $2.5 billion in 1980.

Thus private giving would have to double over the next 5 years to make up for the loss of Federal funds.

Experts at the [c]onference [b]oard suggest that, far from private agencies being able to pick up the slack, many of the agencies will be unable to survive. As one expert has said, "There could be a Darwinian struggle for survival."

* * *

A major effort is being made to bring the corporations of this country into the process of meeting the needs of people of our society. This amendment will facilitate that effort, by raising the limit on corporation contributions to charity. It will encourage companies to respond to the variety of different needs of the people of our country.

Earlier this week, an amendment was adopted to this bill to permit individuals who take the standard deduction to deduct their gifts to charity.[7] That amendment received the over-whelming support of the Senate, and it will encourage individuals to increase their contributions to charities. The amendment I have offered will provide a similar incentive to corporations.

If we are to respond to the challenge of the administration, and seek the support of the private sector in the effort to meet the basic needs of our society, then this is an appropriate amendment to encourage the private sector to do so.[8]

(e)   Specifics of Law Revision

The Act expands the limitation on deductible charitable contributions by corporations, to allow such contributions to be annually deductible to the extent of 10 percent of a corpo-

[7]See Chapter 2 § 1.
[8]127 Cong. Rec. S 8352 (daily ed. July 24, 1981).

ration's taxable income rather than 5 percent of a corporation's taxable income. The Act made no revision in the special definition of "taxable income" or in the carryover rules.

Other provisions of the Act operate to reduce corporations' "taxable income," such as the tax rate reductions and more liberal depreciation allowances. Consequently, the amount deductible—notwithstanding the new ten percent limitaion—is correspondingly circumscribed.

Also, this provision does not expand the deduction against unrelated business income for charitable contributions, which remains at 5 percent (Code § 512(b)(10)).

## § 2.4   Charitable Contribution Deduction for Gifts of Newly Manufactured Equipment to Colleges and Universities for Research

(a)   Summary of Law Revision

Qualifying contributions by a corporation of newly manufactured equipment to a college or university for research or experimentation are deductible, subject to certain limitations (Act § 222).

(b)   Effective Date

This law change became effective on August 13, 1981, and applies to qualified contributions made after that date.

(c)   Prior Law

Under general tax law requirements, the amount of the charitable deduction for a contribution of appreciated ordinary income property is limited to the amount of the taxpayer's basis in the property (Code §§ 170(e)(1) and 1221(1)). This rule generally applies to contributions by a corporation of its inventory, thereby resulting in a small deduction for such contributions.

The law antecedent to the Act provided an exception to these rules, in that a higher deduction is available for corporate contributions of certain property for use in the care of the needy, the ill, or infants (Code § 170(e)(3)). This deduction may not exceed the lesser of (1) an amount equal to one-half of the appreciation in the value of the property plus the taxpayer's basis in the property or (2) an amount equal to twice the taxpayer's basis in the property.

### (d)  Reason for Revision

The purpose of this new charitable deduction is to provide an incentive for increased support by corporations of higher education-based research.

### (e)  Specifics of Law Revision

The Act provides for a deduction for corporations for qualified contributions of newly manufactured ordinary-income property to a college or university for research or experimentation, including research training (Code § 170(e)(4)).

A "qualified research contribution" eligible for this deduction is a gift by a corporation from its inventory (Code § 1221(1)) where the following seven criteria are satisfied: (1) the recipient is an institution of higher education (Code § 3304(f)) that is a tax-exempt educational organization (Code § 170(b)(1)(A)(ii)), (2) the property is constructed by the donor, (3) the contribution is made within two years from the date the construction of the property is substantially completed, (4) the original use of the property is by the donee, (5) the property is scientific equipment or apparatus substantially all of the use of which by the donee is for research or experimentation (Code § 174), or for research training, in the United States in physical or biological sciences, (6) the property is not transferred by the donor in exchange for money, other property, or services, and (7) the donor receives from the donee a written statement representing that its use and disposition of the property will be in accordance with the requirements of criteria (5) and (6).

This deduction may not exceed the lesser of (1) an amount equal to one-half of the appreciation in the value of the property plus the taxpayer's basis in the property or (2) an amount equal to twice the taxpayer's basis in the property.

## § 2.5   Charitable Contribution Deduction for Gifts of Copyrightable Art Works

(a)   Summary of Law Revision

A charitable contribution deduction, for estate and gift tax purposes, is allowed for a transfer of a work of art to a qualified charitable organization, irrespective of whether the copyright therein itself is simultaneously transferred to the charitable organization (Act § 423).

(b)   Effective Date

This law change is effective with respect to the estates of decedents dying, and transfers, after December 31, 1981.

(c)   Prior Law

Where a transfer to a charitable organization is made of an interest which is less than the donor's entire interest in the property, a charitable deduction is not allowable unless the gift of the "split interest" is made in certain specified forms (Code §§ 2055 (e)(2), 2522(c)(2)).

An original work of art and its copyright are interests in the same property. Consequently, a charitable contribution deduction is not allowed for the transfer of an original work of art to charity if the copyright therein is retained by the donor or is transferred to a recipient that is not a charity.

(d)   Reason for Revision

Congress decided to facilitate the deductible contribution (for gift and estate tax purposes) of works of art to charity where the copyright does not likewise pass to charity.

(e)   Specifics of Law Revision

For purposes of the estate and gift tax charitable contribution deduction, where a donor or decedent makes a qualified contribution of a copyrightable work of art, the work of art and its copyright are treated as separate properties (Code §§ 2055(e)(4), 2522(c)(3)). Thus, the transfer to charity of a work of art without the simultaneous transfer of the copyright therein is considered a transfer of the transferor's entire interest in the property.

A "qualified contribution" is a transfer of property to a qualified organization if the use of the property by the organization is related to the tax-exempt purpose or function of the organization.

A "qualified organization" is any charitable, educational, scientific, religious, health, or like organization (Code § 501(c)(3)) other than a private foundation (Code § 509(a)). For this purpose, a private operating foundation (Code § 4942(j)(3)) is a qualified organization.

## § 2.6 Qualification of Income Interests for Marital Deductions

(a)   Summary of Law Revision

The transfer of an income interest created by a qualified charitable remainder trust qualifies for the gift and estate tax marital deduction (Act § 403).

(b)   Effective Date

This law change becomes effective for gifts made or transfers effected by reason of decedents dying after December 31, 1981.

(c)   Prior Law

A charitable remainder trust is a form of split-interest trust, whereby income and remainder interests are created (Code § 664). This type of trust is a vehicle for making a so-called deferred gift, in that the donor receives a current charitable contribution deduction for the value of the remainder interest that will pass to charity.

The charitable organization-remainderman may be any type of charitable organization. The term of the trust may be for a period of years not in excess of 20 or for the life or lives of the income beneficiary or beneficiaries, who must be living at the time of the creation of the trust.

A charitable remainder trust may be one of two forms: the annuity trust or the unitrust.

A charitable remainder annuity trust is a trust from which a "sum certain" must be paid, at least annually, to one or more income beneficiaries who must be as above-described, over a permissible term. If an income beneficiary or beneficiaries is other than an individual or individuals, at least one of such persons must not be a charitable organization. The required sum certain must be at least 5 percent of the initial net fair market value of all of the property placed in trust.

A charitable remainder unitrust is a trust from which a "fixed percentage" of the net fair market value of its assets, valued annually, must be paid, at least annually, to one or more income beneficiaries who must be as above-described, over a permissible term. This value may be determined on any one date during the trust's tax year or by averaging the value on several dates, although the method selected must be consistently employed. The required fixed percentage must be at least 5 percent of the net fair market value of the assets, valued annually.

The value of the remainder interest in a charitable remainder annuity trust is ascertained by subtracting the value of the annuity from the value of the property transferred.

The value of the remainder interest in a charitable remainder unitrust is ascertained by subtracting the value of the income payment (using the required fixed percentage even through the donor elects an income-only interest) from the value of the property transferred.

The income interest created for a spouse as the result of a charitable remainder trust gift does not qualify for the marital deduction.

(d)   Reason for Revision

An inequity was potentially created when the estate and gift tax marital deductions were converted to unlimited deductions.[9]

Thus, under the new rules, a decedent's estate could be left to his or her surviving spouse, with no estate or gift tax. Or a decedent's estate could be left outright to one or more charitable organizations, with no estate or gift tax. Likewise, a combi-

[9]See Chapter 4 § 2.

nation of distributions of a decedent's estate to the surviving spouse and outright to charity would result in no estate or gift tax.

However, without this revision, the life interest created for a spouse by reason of the making of a charitable remainder trust gift would not qualify for the marital deductions—even though the only beneficiaries are the spouse and the charitable organization. This was viewed as a penalty to the donor who selected a deferred charitable gift rather than an outright charitable gift.

(e)   Specifics of Law Revision

An income interest for a spouse created by reason of the making of a charitable gift by means of a charitable remainder trust qualifies for the estate and gift tax marital deductions (Code §§ 2056(b)(8), 2523(g)).

The surviving spouse of the decedent and/or donor must be the only noncharitable beneficiary of the trust. Also, the trust must fully qualify as a charitable remainder annuity trust or charitable remainder unitrust (Code § 664).

The new law does not contain any rule specifically referencing any other form of remainder interest gift to charity by which an income interest in a spouse is created. However, the new rules do create circumstances where a life estate in property in a spouse can qualify for the marital deduction (so-called qualifying terminable interests). Under this rule, a surviving spouse has a qualifying income interest for life where (1) the surviving spouse is entitled to all the income from the property, payable annually or at more frequent intervals, and (2) no person has a power to appoint any part of the property to any person other than the surviving spouse. Applicability of these provisions must be made by election of the executor or executrix (Code §§ 2056(b)(7), 2523(f)).

Certain legislative history of the Act supports the proposition that these general rules provide the basis for qualification for the marital deductions of income interests for spouses created by means of remainder interest giving to charity other than by charitable remainder trusts, namely, for income interests created by gifts by means of pooled income funds (Code § 642(c)(5)) and of charitable remainders in personal residences and farms (Code § 170(f)(3)(B)).[10] Such interests would, to qualify for the marital deductions, have to constitute "qualified terminable interests" and meet the other requirements as discussed including the election. (In this instance, the property involved would be part of the gross estate of the surviving spouse, with the estate tax charitable deduction available for the property passing to charity.) It is not clear whether this new rule affects the prior law in this regard concerning interests in charitable gift annuities created by wills.

## § 2.7   Investment Tax Credit for Rehabilitation of Historic Structures

### (a)   Summary of Law Revision

An investment tax credit is available for the expenses of rehabilitating a certified historic structure and the definition of such a structure is modified (Act § 212).[11]

### (b)   Effective Date

Generally, this law change applies to expenditures made after December 31, 1981. However, where rehabilitation expenditures on a qualified historic structure are incurred both before and after January 1, 1981, the pre-1982 expenditures can qualify for the preexisting investment tax credit or the five-year amortization rule, while expenditures on and after January 1, 1982, can qualify for the new investment tax credit.

### (c)   Prior Law

The tax incentives for the rehabilitation of a building (which has to be at least 20 years old) are a 10 percent investment tax

[10]H. Rep. No. 97–201, 97th Cong., 1st Sess. (1981) at 162; remarks of Steven D. Symms (R-Idaho) at 127 Cong. Rec. S 8346 (daily ed. July 24, 1981).

[11]An expenditure qualifying for an investment tax credit is not a gift qualifying for a deduction but this discussion is included in this chapter because the credit is a form of tax motivation designed to foster an objective that, in some contexts, is "charitable."

credit (Code § 46(a)(2)) (and additional energy credit) or an amortization allowance for expenditures over a 60-month period (Code § 191). The credit does not reduce the basis of the property for purposes of depreciation. The amortization approach is allowable only for rehabilitation of a certified historic structure.

A tax credit is not available for a certified historic structure if approval of the rehabilitation is not obtained from the Secretary of the Interior.

(d)    Reason for Revision

Congress decided it was appropriate to increase the extent of the tax motivation for the rehabilitation of buildings.

(e)    Specifics of Law Revision

The 10 percent regular investment tax credit (and the additional energy credit) and the 60-month amortization provision for certified historic rehabilitation expenditures are repealed. They are replaced by a three-tier investment credit (Code § 46(a)(2)(F)). The credit is 15 percent for structures at least 30 years old, 20 percent for structures at least 40 years old, and 25 percent for certified historic structures. There is no credit for rehabilitation of a building less than 30 years old.

The 15 and 20 percent credits are limited (as under prior law) to nonresidential buildings. However, the 25 percent credit for certified historic rehabilitation is available for both nonresidential and residential buildings. These credits are available only if the taxpayer elects to use the straight-line method of cost recovery for rehabilitation expenditures.

Also, there must be a substantial rehabilitation of the building to qualify for the credit. A building has been substantially rehabilitated if (1) the rehabilitation expenditures during the 24-month period ending on the last day of the tax year exceed the greater of (a) the adjusted basis of the property as of the first day of the 24-month period or (b) $5,000 or (2) it meets the requirements of test (1) by substituting 60 months for 24 months. The 60-month alternative is available only if there is a written set of architectural plans and specifications for all phases of the rehabilitation and a reasonable expectation that all phases of the rehabilitation will be completed.[12]

(For rehabilitation tax credits other than the credit for certified historic rehabilitations, the basis of the property must be reduced by the amount of the credit allowed. If subsequently there is a recapture of the credit, the resulting increase in tax (or adjustment in carrybacks and carryovers) will increase the basis of the building immediately before the recapture event.)

The prior law rule denying an investment tax credit for property leased to tax-exempt organizations (Code § 48(a)(4)) or governmental units (Code § 48(a)(5)) is inapplicable to the portion of the basis of the building attributable to qualified rehabilitation expenditures.

A new rule (Code § 48(g)(3)) treats a building in a historic district as a certified historic structure unless the taxpayer obtains a certification to the contrary from the Secretary of the Interior. This approach reverses the prior law rule under which a building in a historic district is not a certified historic structure unless the Secretary of the Interior takes action to designate the property as being of historic significance to the district.

## § 2.8   Revision of Rules Concerning Certain Transfers of Real Property for Conservation Purposes

(a)   Summary of Law Revision

The definition of the term "certified historic structure" is revised to eliminate the requirement of a certification by the

---

[12] Under the law prior to enactment of the Act, buildings constructed or reconstructed at the site of a demolished or substantially altered certified historic structure must be depreciated using the straight-line method (Code § 167 (n)). Demolition costs must be capitalized as part of the basis of land and thus may not be deducted as a loss or depreciated (Code § 280B). The Act repeals Code § 167(n) but retains Code § 280B, applicable to uses after July 29, 1980, in tax years ending after that date (Act § 214).

Secretary of the Interior that the property is of historic significance to a registered historic district (Act § 212).

(b)   Effective Date

This law change becomes effective for tax years beginning after December 31, 1981.

(c)   Prior Law

In 1980, Congress substantially revised the law concerning the deductibility of charitable contributions of remainder interests in real property for conservation purposes.

The general rule is that deductible gifts of remainder interests can be accomplished only where the interests are conveyed by means of a charitable remainder trust or pooled income fund (Code § 170(f)(2)(A), (3)(A)). One of the exceptions to this rule is the qualified gift of a remainder interest exclusively for conservation purposes (Code § 170(f)(3)(B)(iii)).

The formal term now is a "qualified conservation contribution." Such a gift has three basic elements: it must be a contribution (1) of a qualified real property interest, (2) to a qualified organization, (3) exclusively for conservation purposes.

To be a "qualified real property interest," an interest in real property can be the entire interest of the donor in the property (other than a so-called qualified mineral interest), a remainder interest, or "a restriction (granted in perpetuity) on the use which may be made of the real property." A "qualified mineral interest" is an interest in subsurface oil, gas, or other minerals, and the right of access to such minerals.

The last of the three categories of contributions includes, and replaces, the prior category of gifts covering a lease on, option to purchase, or easement with respect to real property granted in perpetuity (pre-1980 Code § 170(f)(3)(B)(iii)). This revised terminology thus encompasses easements and other interests in real property that under state law have similar attributes (such as a restrictive covenant).

The term "conservation purpose" is given a manifold definition embracing three basic objectives, only one of which need be satisfied.

First, the term includes the "preservation of land areas for outdoor recreation by, or for the education of, the general public." Second, the term "conservation purpose" means the protection of relatively natural habitats of fish, wildlife, plants, or a similar ecosystem. Third, "conservation purpose" includes the "preservation of open space (including farmland and forest land)" where the preservation is "for the scenic enjoyment of the general public," "pursuant to a clearly delineated Federal, State, or local governmental conservation policy, and will yield a significant public benefit," or "the preservation of an historically important land area or a certified historic structure."

The term "historically important land area" includes independently significant land areas (such as a Civil War battlefield) and historic sites and related land areas, the physical or environmental features of which contribute to the historic or cultural importance and continuing integrity of certified historic structures or historic districts. The integrity of a certified historic structure may be protected under this rule by perpetual restrictions on the development of such a related land area.

The term "certified historic structure" is defined in the statute as any "building, structure, or land area" which is listed in the National Register, or is located in a "restricted historic district" (Code § 191(d)(2)) and is certified by the Secretary of the Interior to the Secretary of the Treasury as being of historic significance to the district. A structure is a "structure" for this purpose whether or not it is depreciable, so, for example, an easement on a private residence may qualify. Also, a structure may be a "certified historic structure" if it satisfies the certification requirements either at the time of the transfer or at the due date (including extensions) for filing the donor's federal income tax return for the year in which the contribution was made.

Not only must a contribution be for a conservation purpose, it must be made "exclusively" for conservation purposes. This requirement is not satisfied unless the conservation purpose is protected in perpetuity. The contribution must involve legally enforceable restrictions on any interest in the property retained by the donor so as to prevent uses of the retained interest inconsistent with the conservation purposes. In the case of a contribution of a remainder interest, the contribution will not qualify if the tenants, whether they are tenants for life or a term of years, can use the property in a manner that diminishes the conservation values that are intended to be protected by the contribution. Further, this requirement is not met if the contribution, while accomplishing one of the conservation purposes, would allow uses of the property that would be destructive of other significant conservation interests. This requirement does not, however, prohibit uses of the property (such as the selective cutting of timber or farming) if, under the circumstances, the uses are not destructive of significant conservation interests.

A charitable organization must be a "qualified organization" to be the recipient of a deductible gift of a conservation contribution in the form of a remainder interest. In essence, such a donee must be a publicly supported charity or a governmental unit. Specifically, such qualified donees are (1) publicly supported charitable organizations (Code §§ 170(b)(1)(A)(vi) and 509(a)(1), or Code § 509(a)(2)), (2) units of government (Code §§ 170(b)(1)(A)(v) and 509(a)(1)), or (3) charitable organizations that are supportive of and controlled by publicly supported charities or governmental units (Code § 509(a)(3)). Thus, a charitable contribution deduction is not available for a gift of a conservation contribution in the form of a remainder interest made to an entity classified as a church, university, college, school, hospital or private foundation, unless it is also described in at least one of these categories.

(d)   Reason for Revision

The definition of the term "certified historic structure" was revised to liberalize the term and thus expand the scope of the tax motivation for the transfer by gift of such property.

(e)   Specifics of Law Revision

A new provision defines the term "certified historic structure" (Code § 48(g)(3)(A)) as "any building (and its structural components) which (i) is listed in the National Register, or (ii) is located in a registered historic district and is certified by the Secretary of the Interior to the Secretary [of the Treasury] as being of historic significance to the district."

A "registered historic district" (Code § 48(g)(3)(B)) is "(i) any district listed in the National Register, and (ii) any district (I) which is designated under a statute of the appropriate State or local government, if such statute is certified by the Secretary of the Interior to the Secretary [of the Treasury] as containing criteria which will substantially achieve the purpose of preserving and rehabilitating buildings of historic significance to the district, and (II) which is certified by the Secretary of the Interior to the Secretary [of the Treasury] as meeting substantially all of the requirements for the listing of districts in the National Register."

This new definition of the term "certified historic structure" is presumably to be used for the charitable giving rules (Code § 170(f)(3)(B)(iii)), since the prior definition used the term as it was defined in the amortization allowance rules (Code § 191)[13] and those rules are repealed by the Act (Act § 212 (d)(1)). However, the word "presumably" is used in the foregoing definition in that the Act fails to contain a conforming amendment regarding the charitable giving rules (Act § 212 (d)(2)).

## § 2.9   Special Estate Tax Credit

(a)   Summary of Law Revision

A special credit against estate taxes is available for a certain transfer to the Smithsonian Institution (Act § 429).

(b)   Effective Date

The transfer, to qualify for this credit, must be made within 30 days after enactment of the Act (which was August 13, 1981).

(c)   Prior Law

The law antedating this revision did not provide for the relief afforded by the new provision.

(d)   Reasons for Revision

The law antedating this revision did not provide for the relief afforded by the new provision.

[13]See § 7 hereof.

(e)  Specifics of Law Revision

The Act provides that, upon timely transfer to the Smithsonian Institution of all right, title, and interests held by the Dorothy Meserve Kunhardt trust and the estate of Dorothy Meserve Kunhardt in the collection of approximately 7,250 Mathew Brady glass plate negatives and the Alexander Gardner imperial portrait print of Abraham Lincoln, there shall be allowed as a credit, effective as of the date upon which the return was due to be filed, against the estate tax on the estate an amount equal to the lesser of (1) the estate tax, (2) the fair market value of the negatives and the print, or (3) $700,000.

# 3

# The New Tax-Exempt
# Organizations Rules

## § 3.1  Introduction

Unlike most comprehensive tax revision laws, the Act does not contain a great amount of changes directly affecting the law of tax-exempt organizations. For example, no new category of tax-exempt organization was created, no general revision in the public charity rules was adopted, and no adjustment in the law concerning the tax treatment of unrelated business income was enacted.

Nonetheless, the Act contains a variety of new rules relating to tax-exempt organizations.

The principal revision made by the Act in this regard was a modification of the private foundation payout requirement (§ 2 hereof), which also affects the definition of a private operating foundation (§ 3).

Another important revision is the introduction of rules concerning the types of tax-exempt organizations that can qualify as entities to participate with corporations in contract research that is eligible for a tax credit (§ 4). Of interest are the new rules governing college- and university-related funds that can be converted to private foundations if the new tax treatment is elected.

Other provisions of the Act pertaining to tax-exempt organizations reduce the tax rates on unrelated business income (§ 5), expand the exemption from the windfall profit tax (§ 6), reduce the tax rates applicable to principal campaign committees (§ 7), extend the rules concerning prepaid legal services programs (§ 8), provide an unlimited gift tax exclusion for tuition and medical care payments (§ 9), and continue the moratorium on the issuance of fringe benefit regulations (§ 10).

## § 3.2    Private Foundation Annual Payout Requirements

(a)    Summary of Law Revision

A private foundation must annually distribute for charitable purposes an amount equal to its minimum investment return (Act § 823).

(b)    Effective Date

This law change becomes effective for tax years beginning after December 31, 1981.

(c)    Prior Law

A private foundation (other than a private operating foundation) is required to distribute at least a minimum amount of funds for charitable purposes (Code § 4942). As originally enacted in 1969, this rule requires a foundation to distribute all of its adjusted net income (less certain taxes) for its exempt purposes in respect of each tax year. However, under this requirement, if, in any year, the net income of a private foundation is not equal to the mandatory payout requirement, a portion of the foundation's principal has to be combined with its income so that the total annual distribution (principal and income) equals at least 5 percent of the value of the foundation's noncharitable assets. This amount thereby determined is the "minimum investment return" and the amount which must be distributed is the "distributable amount."

A foundation's minimum investment return for any tax year

(as defined in Code § 4942(e)(1)) is the amount determined by multiplying (1) the excess of the aggregate fair market value of all assets of the foundation, other than those being used or held for use directly in carrying out the foundation's exempt purpose, over the amount of the acquisition indebtedness with respect to the assets (without regard to the tax year in which the indebtedness was incurred), by (2) 5 percent. The aggregate fair market value of all assets of a foundation must include the average of the fair market values on a monthly basis of securities for which market quotations are readily available, the average of the foundation's cash balances on a monthly basis, and the fair market value of all other noncharitable assets for the period of time during the year for which such assets are held by the foundation.

The following assets are not taken into account in determining minimum investment return: (1) any future interest (such as a vested or contingent remainder, whether legal or equitable) of a foundation in the income or corpus of any real or personal property until all intervening interests in, and the rights to the actual possession or enjoyment of, such property have expired, or, although not actually reduced to the foundation's possession, until such future interest has been constructively received by the foundation, as, for example, where it has been credited to the foundation's account, set apart for the foundation, or otherwise made available so that the foundation may acquire it at any time or could have acquired it if notice of intention to acquire had been given, (2) the assets of an estate until such time as such assets are distributed to the foundation or, due to a prolonged period of administration, such estate is considered terminated for federal income tax purposes, (3) present interests in any trust created and funded by another person, (4) any pledge of money or property, whether or not the pledge is legally enforceable, and (5) any assets used or held for use directly in carrying out the foundation's exempt purposes.

An asset is "used (or held for use) directly in carrying out the foundation's exempt purpose" (under Code § 4942(e)(1)(A)) if the asset is actually used by the foundation in the carrying out of the charitable, educational, or other purpose which gives rise to the exempt status of the foundation, or if the foundation owns the asset and establishes to the satisfaction of the I.R.S. that its immediate use for exempt purposes is not practical and that definite plans exist to begin such use within a reasonable period of time. Consequently, assets which are held for the production of income or for investment (for example, stocks, bonds, interest-bearing notes, endowment funds, or, generally, leased real estate) must be taken into account in determining minimum investment return. Where property is used both for exempt purposes and for other purposes, it is considered to be used exclusively for exempt purposes where such exempt use represents 95 percent or more of the total use; otherwise, a reasonable allocation between exempt and nonexempt uses must be made.

### (d)  Reason for Revision

As originally enacted in 1969, the mandatory payout requirement did not forbid a foundation from making low-yield investments, such as investments in growth stock or nonproductive land, if it wished. However, if the foundation did so, it periodically may have had to sell some assets to meet the distribution requirements or distribute property to public charities in partial satisfaction of the requirements. In either instance, the foundation would be chipping away at its corpus—its endowment—thereby merely postponing the day when its heedless investment policies caused its decline and then extinction. It is for this reason that the supporters of the mandatory distribution rules as finally developed in 1969 abandoned the "death knell" approach to foundations—adopted by the Senate in its version of the tax reform legislation—by which foundations would be forced to terminate after a stated period of years. The mandatory payout requirement was seen as a stratagem for eliminating foundations with foolhardy or private interest investment philosophies. However, during the 1970s, the real value of most foundations' assets was eroded and the income yield of many debt investments rose dramatically, so the total income payout requirement was abandoned to enable foundations to revise their investment strategies to assure their continued existence.

(e)   Specifics of Law Revision

The Act reduces the payout requirement for private foundations, by requiring only that the minimum investment return be distributed (Code § 4942(d)(1)). Thus, the income distribution requirement was dropped.

## § 3.3   Modification of Definition of a Private Operating Foundation

(a)   Summary of Law Revision

The definition of the term "private operating foundation" is revised in conformance with the revision of the private foundation payout requirement (Act § 823).

(b)   Effective Date

This law change is applicable to tax years beginning after December 31, 1981.

(c)   Prior Law

Private operating foundations, while not statutorily defined until the enactment of Code § 4942(j)(3) in 1969, have long been recognized as non-publicly supported organizations which devote most of their earnings and much of their assets directly to the conduct of their exempt purposes, as opposed to merely making grants to other organizations.

A private operating foundation must meet the income test of Code § 4942(j)(3)(A). This means that the foundation must expend substantially all of its adjusted net income, in the form of qualifying distributions, directly for the active conduct of its exempt activities. Thus, the funds expended must be used by the foundation itself rather than by or through one or more grantee organizations.

The making or awarding of grants, scholarships, or similar payments to individual beneficiaries to support active exempt programs will qualify the grantor as a private operating foundation only if it maintains some significant involvement in the programs.

The term "significant involvement" has two basic meanings. Such involvement is present where payments to accomplish the foundation's exempt purpose are made directly and without the assistance of an intervening organization or agency, and the foundation maintains a staff (for example, administrators or researchers) which supervises and directs the exempt activities on a continuing basis. To utilize this meaning of the term, the foundation must have as an exempt purpose the relief of poverty or human distress and its exempt purposes must be designed to ameliorate conditions among a poor or distressed class of persons or in an area subject to poverty or natural disaster (for example, providing food or clothing to indigents or residents of a disaster area). Such involvement is also present where the foundation has developed some specialized skills, expertise, or involvement in a particular discipline, and it maintains a staff which supervises or conducts programs or activities which support its work, if the foundation makes grants or other payments to individuals to encourage their involvement in its field of interest and in some segment of the activities it carries on. An example of the latter would be grants to engage in scientific research projects under the general direction and supervision of the foundation.

The income test requires "substantially all" (that is, at least 85 percent) of the foundation's adjusted net income to be devoted to the active conduct of an exempt function. Qualification under the income test is not lost if the foundation makes grants to organizations or engages in other activities with the remainder of its adjusted net income and other funds.

Amounts paid to acquire or maintain assets used directly in the conduct of the foundation's exempt activities constitute qualifying distributions. Examples of such expenditures are payments for the operating assets of a museum, public park, or historic site. Reasonable administrative expenses (for example, salaries and travel outlays) and other necessary operating costs are likewise the subject of qualifying distributions. However, administrative expenses and operating costs which are not attributable to exempt activities, such as expenses in connection with the production of investment income, do not qualify. Expenses attributable to both exempt and nonexempt activities must be allocated to each activity on a reasonable and consistently applied basis.

In addition to the income test, to qualify as an operating foundation, a private foundation must satisfy an "assets test," an "endowment test," or a "support test."

### (d)  Reason for Revision

This law change was occasioned by reason of the revision in the law concerning the private foundation payout requirement.[1]

### (e)  Specifics of Revision

The requirement of the private operating foundation income test that such a foundation's qualifying distributions (Code § 4942(g)(1) or (2)) be equal to substantially all of its adjusted net income (Code § 4942(f)) has been replaced with a requirement that the payout be equal to substantially all of the lesser of its adjusted net income or its minimum investment return.[2] Consequently, the amount that need be distributed by a private operating foundation may be less than 85 percent of its adjusted net income.

For a private operating foundation, its minimum investment return is 5 percent (the same as the standard private foundation minimum investment return) of its noncharitable assets.[3] Under the new definition, therefore, the amount that must be annually expended by an operating foundation for the active conduct of charitable activities is one of the following: (1) where the amount equal to eighty-five percent of an operating foundation's adjusted net income is less than the applicable portion of

---

[1] § 2 hereof.

[2] The term "minimum investment return" is discussed in § 2 hereof.

[3] As noted, a private operating foundation must, in addition to satisfying the income test, meet one of three other tests. One of these is the "endowment" test requiring a foundation to normally make qualifying distributions directly for the active conduct of charitable activities equal to at least two-thirds of the minimum investment return (Code § 4942(j)(3)(B)(ii)). This payout amount, which is $3\frac{1}{3}$ percent ($\frac{2}{3}$ of five percent), remains unaffected by the new requirements.

minimum investment return (4.25 percent), the foundation's payout requirement would be the same as under prior law, and (2) where the amount equal to eighty-five percent of an operating foundation's adjusted net income is greater than the applicable portion of minimum investment return, the amount that must be distributed is equal to 4.25 percent of the value of the noncharitable assets of the foundation.

The Act adds a cryptic sentence at the end of the definition of private operating foundation, reading: "Notwithstanding the provisions of subparagraph (A) [the "income test" provision], if the qualifying distributions . . . of an organization for the taxable year exceed the minimum investment return for the taxable year, clause (ii) of subparagraph (A) [the new substantially-all-of-minimum-investment-return limitation on the payout amount] shall not apply unless substantially all of such qualifying distributions are made directly for the active conduct of the activities constituting the purpose or function for which it is organized and operated." This means that the new—and in this case lower —ceiling on the required operating foundation payout amount will not be applicable if the foundation's qualifying distributions in excess of the year's minimum investment return are not expended in conformance with the income test requirements. That is, in such an instance, the prior law applies, namely, the requirement becomes—once again—a minimum of eighty-five percent of adjusted net income must go to the active conduct of the charitable activities.

Moreover, this rule is intended to expand the "substantially all" test to embrace, not just an amount equal to adjusted net income, but all amounts expended in the form of qualifying distributions (cash and/or property). The design of this rule is to preclude the opportunity for a private nonoperating foundation to qualify for operating foundation status while funding substantial grant programs out of distributions that exceed an amount equal to 4.25 percent of the value of noncharitable assets. A private operating foundation that engages in such a practice will likely lose its operating foundation classification for the year involved.[4]

[4]The entire rule does not become operative until a foundation's annual distributions exceed its minimum investment return. Where

As an illustration, assume a private operating foundation (X) with $500,000 of noncharitable assets, operating on the calendar year basis, with annual adjusted net income of $50,000 (ten percent of the assets). For 1981, X is required to expend for the active conduct of its charitable activities at least $42,500 (85 percent of $50,000). For 1982 (assuming the same value of assets and same income), the mandatory payout for X would be considerably smaller, namely, $21,250, that being the lesser of substantially all of adjusted net income ($42,500) or substantially all of minimum investment return (85 percent of five percent of $500,000, or $21,-250). Concerning the new rule relating to "excess" qualifying distributions, assume that in 1982 X distributed $30,000. This amount is in excess of the minimum investment return ($25,000), so the new rule is activated. The intention of the new rule is to require—to assure continuity of X's operating foundation status—that X expend at least $25,500 (85 percent of $30,000) for the active conduct of its exempt activities. In fact, however, the new rule does not work that way. Suppose that X expended $25,200 of the $30,000 (84 percent) for the active conduct of its exempt activities. This would trigger the new rule, because the actual distributions for the active conduct of exempt activities ($25,200) exceed the minimum investment return ($25,000). Since the amount expended in 1982 for the active conduct of its exempt activi-

---

the rule is activated, the new substantially-all-of-minimum-investment-return limitation on the payout amount (Code § 4942(j)(3)(A)(ii)) will not apply unless substantially all of the total distributions meet the income test. If that test is thus met, the new limitation applies (although, in that context, it does not matter, since the larger actual payout meets the substantially all test continued from prior law). However, if that test is not met, because substantially all of the total distributions do not meet the income test requirement, the new limitation does not apply. This would leave only the eighty-five-percent-of-adjusted-net-income test (Code § 4942(j)(3)(A)(i)), which—since it applies only to adjusted net income, an amount that may be lower than "qualifying distributions"—may not cause the desired result of imposing the eighty-five percent test on all the distributions of the year, and may cause the operating foundation to be in violation of the income test payout requirements.

ties ($25,200) is less than 85 percent of its total distributions (of $30,000), the minimum investment return limitation is eliminated, resulting in a payout requirement of $42,500. This requirement is not satisfied ($25,200 < $42,500) nor is the intended result of requiring X to expend $25,500 of the $30,000 for the active conduct of exempt activities, leaving the new rule not operating as intended and X in violation of the payout rule.

Thus, this new rule carries with it a substantial sanction. If it is violated (namely, if 85 percent of total qualifying distributions in excess of minimum investment return are not devoted to the active conduct of charitable activities), the payout requirement probably cannot be met, and the organization will likely lose its operating foundation status for the year involved and become classified as a private foundation.

## § 3.4    Tax Credit for Research and Experimentation

### (a)    Summary of Law Revision

A 25 percent tax credit is available for certain research and experimental expenditures paid in carrying on a trade or business (Act § 221).

### (b)    Effective Date

The new rules apply to amounts paid or incurred after June 30, 1981, and before January 1, 1986.

### (c)    Prior Law

Under preexisting law, a taxpayer may elect to deduct currently the amount of research or experimental expenditures incurred in connection with the taxpayer's trade or business or may elect to amortize certain research costs over a period of at least 60 months (Code § 174). These rules apply to the costs of research conducted by the taxpayer and, in general, to expenses paid for research conducted on behalf of the taxpayer by a research firm, university, or the like.

No tax credit was available for research expenses.

(d)   Reason for Revision

The purpose of this new tax credit is to provide an incentive for the increased conduct of research and experimentation.

(e)   Specifics of Law Revision

The Act provides a 25 percent tax credit for certain research and experimental expenditures paid in carrying on a trade or business (Code § 44F). The credit is allowable to the extent that current-year expenditures exceed the average amount of research expenditures in a base period (generally, the preceding three tax years). Subject to certain exclusions, the term "qualified research" used for purposes of the credit is the same as that used for purposes of the special deduction rules (Code § 174).

Research expenditures qualifying for this new credit consist of two basic types: "in-house research" expenses and "contract research" expenses.

In-house research expenditures are those for research wages and supplies, along with certain lease or other charges for research use of computers, laboratory equipment, and the like. Contract research expenditures are 65 percent of amounts paid to another person (for example, a research firm or university) for research.

A tax credit is also available for 65 percent of an amount paid by a corporation to a qualified organization for basic research to be performed by the recipient organization, where the relationship is evidenced by a written research agreement. (Such research is a form of "contract research.") The term "basic research" means "any original investigation for the advancement of scientific knowledge not having a specific commercial objective, except that such term shall not include (A) basic research conducted outside the United States, and (B) basic research in the social sciences or humanities."

For purposes of the rules concerning basic contract research, a "qualified organization" is either (1) an institution of higher education (Code § 3304(f)) that is a tax-exempt educational organization (Code § 170(b)(1)(A)(ii)) or (2) any other type of charitable, educational, scientific, or like tax-exempt organization

(Code § 501(c)(3)) that is organized and operated primarily to conduct scientific research and is not a private foundation (Code § 509(a)).[5]

A special provision allows certain "funds" organized and operated exclusively to make basic research grants to institutions of higher education to be considered as a "qualifying organization," even though the fund does not itself perform the research. To qualify, the fund must be a charitable, educational, scientific, or like tax-exempt organization (Code § 501(c)(3)), not be a private foundation (Code § 509(a)), be established and maintained by an organization that is a public charity and was created prior to July 10, 1981, and make its grants under written research agreements. Moreover, a fund must elect to become such a "qualified fund" and, by making the election, the fund becomes treated as a private foundation, except that the investment income excise tax (Code § 4940) is not applicable.[6]

In general, the conferees, in finalizing the Act, stated that this credit is available only for qualified research expenditures paid by the taxpayer in carrying on a trade or business of the taxpayer. The conferees also stated that the credit is allowable in the case of research joint ventures by taxpayers who otherwise satisfy the "carrying on" test (Code § 162) and who are entitled to the research results.

[5]One of the questions thus posed by this provision is whether private operating foundations (see § 3 hereof) are eligible to participate in this contract research program. Certainly these types of foundations that conduct their own research should be qualified organizations for this purpose, notwithstanding the general prohibition against the involvement of private foundations (Code § 44F(e)(2)(B)(iii)). For purposes of the new provision allowing an estate and gift tax charitable contribution deduction for the transfer of a work of art to a qualified charitable organization, irrespective of whether the copyright therein is simultaneously transferred to the charitable organization (see Chapter 2 § 5), a private operating foundation is expressly included as a qualified organization (Code § 2055(e)(4)(D)) even though "private foundations" are excluded.

[6]Once this election is made, it can be revoked only with the consent of the Internal Revenue Service.

## § 3.5   Reduction in Unrelated Income Tax Rates

(a)   Summary of Law Revision

The tax rates imposed upon the unrelated income of tax-exempt organizations have been reduced (Act §§ 101 and 231).

(b)   Effective Date

These law changes become effective for tax years beginning after December 31, 1981.

(c)   Prior Law

Even though an organization achieves general income tax exemption, it nonetheless remains potentially taxable on any unrelated business income (Code § 501(b)). This tax (as imposed by Code § 511(a)(1)) is levied at corporate rates (Code § 11) or, in the case of charitable trusts (under Code § 511(b)), at individual rates (Code § 1(d)).

The taxation of unrelated income, a feature of the Code since 1950, is based on the concept that the approach is a more effective and workable sanction for authentic enforcement of the law of exempt organizations than total denial of exempt status. It is basically a simple concept: the unrelated business income tax only applies to active business income which arises from activities which are "unrelated" to the organization's exempt purposes.

Prior to enactment of the Tax Reform Act of 1969, the unrelated business income tax applied only to certain tax-exempt organizations, including charitable, educational, some religious, and comparable organizations; labor, agricultural, and horticultural organizations; and business leagues and similar organizations. However, the tax on unrelated business income is now imposed on nearly all exempt organizations, its coverage having been extended by the Tax Reform Act of 1969 (Code § 511(a)(2)(A)). Congress decided to broaden the applicability of the unrelated business income tax for the following reason:

> In recent years, many of the exempt organizations not subject to the unrelated business income tax—such as churches, social clubs, fraternal beneficiary societies, etc.—began to engage in

substantial commercial activity. For example, numerous business activities of churches were brought to the attention of the Congress. Some churches are engaged in operating publishing houses, hotels, factories, radio and TV stations, parking lots, newspapers, bakeries, restaurants, etc. Furthermore, it is difficult to justify taxing a university or hospital which runs a public restaurant or hotel or other business and not tax a country club or lodge engaged in similar activity.[7]

The unrelated business income tax now applies to nearly all exempt organizations, including churches and conventions or associations of churches, social welfare organizations, social clubs, and fraternal societies. This tax applies to any college or university which is an agency or instrumentality of any government or political subdivision thereof, or which is owned or operated by a government or any political subdivision thereof, or by any agency or instrumentality of one or more governments or political subdivisions, and applies to any corporation wholly owned by one or more such colleges or universities (Code § 511(a)(2)(B)). Excepted from the tax are federal government instrumentalities, certain religious and apostolic organizations, farmers' cooperatives, and shipowners' protection and indemnity associations.

The primary objective of the unrelated business income tax is to eliminate a source of unfair competition by placing the unrelated business activities of covered exempt organizations on the same tax basis as the nonexempt business endeavors with which they compete. The House Ways and Means Committee report on the Revenue Act of 1950 observed:

> The problem at which the tax on unrelated business income is directed here is primarily that of unfair competition. The tax-free status of ... [Code § 501] organizations enables them to use their profits tax-free to expand operations, while their competitors can expand only with the profits remaining after taxes.[8]

The Senate Finance Committee reaffirmed this position in the context of enactment of the Tax Reform Act of 1976 when it noted that one "major purpose" of the unrelated income tax "is to make certain that an exempt organization does not commer-

---

[7]Joint Committee on Internal Revenue Taxation, General Explanation of Tax Reform Act of 1969, 91st Cong., 2d Sess. (1970) at 66–67.

[8]H. Rep. No. 2319, 81st Cong., 2d Sess. (1950) at 36. Also S. Rep. No. 2375, 81st Cong., 2d Sess. (1950) at 28.

cially exploit its exempt status for the purpose of unfairly competing with taxpaying organizations."[9]

However, the absence or presence of unfair competition is not among the technical criteria for assessing whether a particular activity is subject to the unrelated business income tax. Thus it is theoretically possible for an exempt organization activity to be wholly uncompetitive with a taxpaying organization activity and nonetheless be treated as an unrelated trade or business. On occasion, the I.R.S. has taken the position that, where an activity constitutes a trade or business and is not substantially related to the performance of exempt functions, there is sufficient likelihood (something akin to an irrebutable presumption) that unfair competition is present.

Under the law antedating these revisions, the corporate income tax is imposed at the following rates:

| Taxable income | Rate (percent) |
| --- | --- |
| Less than $25,000 | 17 |
| 25,000–50,000 | 20 |
| 50,000–75,000 | 30 |
| 75,000–100,000 | 40 |
| Over $100,000 | 46 |

(d)  Reasons for Revision

As Congress adjusts tax rates from time to time, as is its wont, the taxation of unrelated income likewise becomes affected. Undoubtedly, the unrelated income rates payable by most tax-exempt organizations are the corporate rates.

The corporate rate reductions provided by the Act are intended for the benefit of business corporations, as part of the overall program of incentives for economic recovery. The reductions were not enacted for the benefit of tax-exempt organizations.

(e)  Specifics of Law Revision

The Act decreases the tax rates on the two lowest corporate tax brackets, namely, those imposing tax on taxable income below $50,000. The changes will go into effect in 1982 and 1983.

[9]S. Rep. No. 94-938, 94th Cong., 2d Sess. (1976) at 601.

The brackets below $50,000 will be adjusted as follows:

| Taxable income | Rate (percent) |
|---|---|
| In 1982— | |
| Less than $25,000 | 16 |
| $25,000–$50,000 | 19 |
| 1983 and later years | |
| Less than $25,000 | 15 |
| $25,000–$50,000 | 18 |

Thus, for example, the same unrelated income that is taxable at the 17 percent rate in 1981 will be taxable at a 16 percent rate in 1982 and a 15 percent rate in 1983.

## § 3.6    Expansion of Windfall Profit Tax Exemption for Child Care Agencies

(a)    Summary of Law Revision

The existing windfall profit tax exemption for certain tax-exempt organizations is extended to encompass charitable organizations that are organized and operated primarily for the residential placement, care or treatment of delinquent, dependent, orphaned, neglected, or handicapped children (Act § 604).

(b)    Effective Date

This law change is applicable to tax periods beginning after December 31, 1980.

(c)    Prior Law

The Crude Oil Windfall Profit Tax Act of 1980 imposed a windfall profit tax, which is a temporary levy, retroactive to March 1, 1980. The tax applies to the "windfall profit" derived from the sale of domestically produced crude oil. The windfall profit is the selling price of the oil less an adjusted base price and a deduction for state severance taxes on the profit. Taxable oil is classified into one of three "tiers." The tiers differ in several respects, including the tax rate which is applied and the adjusted base price which is used. The rates may be as high as 70 percent.

Oil produced from properties owned by educational institutions and medical facilities is exempt from the windfall profit tax where the properties were held by the organizations on January 21, 1980. These organizations must be tax-exempt as "charitable" entities (Code §§ 170(c)(2) and 501(c)(3)). Educational institutions must also be classified under Code § 170(b)(1)(A)(ii) or (iv). Medical facilities must also be classified under Code § 170(b)(1)(A)(iii). Educational institutions are described as those that maintain a faculty and curriculum and have a regularly enrolled student body at the place where the educational activities are conducted. Related "foundations" for state colleges and universities are included in this description. Medical facilities are described as hospitals and certain medical research organizations (Code § 4994(b)(1)(A)).

Oil produced from interests held by a church (Code § 170(b)(1)(A)(i)) on January 21, 1980, is exempt from the tax—but only if the net proceeds from production of such oil were dedicated to the support of an educational institution or medical facility prior to January 22, 1980. Proceeds from an oil interest received after January 21, 1980, such as a bequest, are not eligible for the exemption.

(d) Reason for Revision

Congress decided it is appropriate to expand the scope of the windfall profit tax exemption for qualifying child care agencies.

(e) Specifics of Law Revision

The existing windfall profit tax exemption for specified charitable and educational organizations and medical facilities is extended to cover oil production attributable to economic interests held by a charitable organization (Code §§ 170(c)(2) and 501(c)(3)) "which is organized and operated primarily for the residential placement, care or treatment of delinquent, dependent, orphaned, neglected, or handicapped children" (Code § 4994(b)(1)(A)(ii)).

To qualify for this exemption, the oil interest must have been held by the organization on January 21, 1980, and at all times thereafter before the last day of the calendar quarter.

If the interest is not held by the organization, the exemption may apply if the interest was held by a church for the benefit of the organization and if all the proceeds from the interest were dedicated on January 21, 1980, and at all times thereafter before the close of the calendar quarter, to the qualifying child care agency.

## § 3.7 Rate of Tax for Principal Campaign Committees

(a)  Summary of Law Revision

The generally applicable corporate income tax rates are applicable to the taxable income of a congressional candidate's principal campaign committee (Act § 128).

(b)  Effective Date

This law change becomes effective for tax years beginning after December 31, 1981.

(c)  Prior Law

Code § 527 provides exemption for the "political organization." Effective with respect to tax years beginning in 1975, Code § 527 statutorily overrides previous I.R.S. determinations on the point, to the effect that an unincorporated campaign committee is not exempt from federal income taxation and must file tax returns showing as gross income interest, dividends, and net gains from the sale of securities and related deductions.

Pursuant to Code § 527(e), a political organization is a party, committee, association, fund, or other organization organized and operated primarily for the purpose of directly or indirectly accepting contributions or making expenditures, or both, for an "exempt function." An exempt function is the function of influencing or attempting to influence the selection, nomination, election, or appointment of any individual to any federal, state, or local public office or office in a political organization, or the election of presidential or vice-presidential electors.

Candidates for election to Congress must designate one "principal campaign committee" to receive contributions and make expenditures on the candidate's behalf.[10] A campaign committee may be designated as a principal campaign committee by only one candidate and a designated committee may not support any other candidate. A statement of designation must be filed with the Federal Election Commission and, as appropriate, with the Clerk of the House or the Secretary of the Senate.

Political organizations are subject (under Code § 527(b)) to the highest rate, rather than the graduated rates, of corporate tax on their "taxable income," which, under Code § 527(c), is their gross income, less "exempt function income" and direct expenses, subject to certain modifications. Exempt function income (under Code § 527(c)(3)) means (1) contributions of money or other property, (2) membership dues, membership fees or assessments from a member of the organization, (3) proceeds from a political fundraising or entertainment event, or (4) proceeds from the sale of political campaign materials, which are not received in the ordinary course of any trade or business, to the extent such amount is segregated for use only for the exempt function of the political organization. A principal item of taxable income is interest.

The highest corporate tax rate is 46 percent for amounts over $100,000.

(d)   Reason for Revision

Congress believed that there is no rationale for taxing principal campaign committees any differently from corporations generally.

(e)   Specifics of Law Revision

This law change causes the generally applicable corporate income tax rates to apply to political organization taxable income of a congressional candidate's principal campaign committee. Thus, in 1982, the lowest rate would be 16 percent as

[10] 2 U.S.C. § 432(e).

to amounts of $25,000 or less,[11] and the highest rate would continue to be 46 percent on amounts over $100,000.

## § 3.8   Qualified Group Legal Services Plans

(a)   Summary of Law Revision

Employer contributions to, and benefits provided under, a qualified group legal services plan are excluded, through December 31, 1984, from an employee's income (Act § 802).

(b)   Effective Date

This law change became effective on August 13, 1981.

(c)   Prior Law

Congress, in adopting the Tax Reform Act of 1976, enacted a category of tax-exempt organization, namely, an entity established to form part of a qualified group legal services plan or plans. This provision is a portion of a overall scheme providing favorable tax treatment of prepaid group legal services provided by employers to their employees. To provide a tax incentive for such plans, Congress has excluded from an employee's income (1) amounts contributed by an employer to a qualified group legal services plan for employees, their spouses, or their dependents and (2) the value of services received by an employee or any amounts paid to an employee under such a plan as reimbursement for legal services for the employee or his or her spouse or dependents (Code § 120(a)). To be a qualified plan, a group legal services plan must fulfill several requirements with regard to its provisions, the employer, and the covered employees.

A qualified group legal services plan must be a separate written plan of an employer for the exclusive benefit of his or her employees or their spouses or dependents. The plan must supply the employees (or their spouses or dependents) with specified benefits consisting of personal (i.e., nonbusiness) legal services through prepayment of, or provision in advance for, all

[11]See Chapter 3 § 2.

or part of an employee's, his or her spouse's, or his or her dependents' legal fees (Code § 120(b)). Also, to be qualified, the group legal services plan must meet requirements of nondiscrimination in contributions or benefits and in eligibility for enrollment (Code § 120(c)).

Amounts contributed by employers under a plan may be paid only (1) to insurance companies, (2) to qualified exempt organizations, (3) as prepayments to providers of legal services under the plan, or (4) to a combination of the foregoing types of eligible payment recipients (Code § 120(c)(5)). The entity referenced in category (2) is the subject of Code § 501(c)(20), described as "an organization or trust created or organized in the United States, the exclusive function of which is to form part of a qualified group legal services plan or plans, within the meaning of section 120." An organization is not to be deprived of exemption by reason of Code § 501(c)(20) because "it provides legal services or indemnification against the cost of legal services unassociated with a qualified group legal services plan" in addition to receiving contributions by reason of Code § 120(c)(5).

To be treated as a qualified group legal services plan, the plan must timely notify the I.R.S. that it is applying for recognition of such status (see Code §§ 120(c)(4), (d)(7)). The provisions concerning these organizations are applicable to tax years beginning after December 31, 1976, and ending before January 1, 1982.

### (d)  Reasons for Revision

Congress decided that the above-described tax treatment for qualified group legal services plans should be continued beyond 1981.

### (e)  Specifics of Law Revision

The expiration date for the exclusion for prepaid legal services which was for tax years ending before January 1, 1982, was revised to extend the exclusion through tax years ending after December 31, 1984.

## § 3.9    Gift Tax Unlimited Exclusion

### (a)    Summary of Law Revision

An unlimited exclusion from the gift tax is available for amounts paid for the benefit of a donee for tuition and certain medical expenses (Act § 441).

### (b)    Effective Date

This law change is effective for transfers made after December 31, 1981.

### (c)    Prior Law

The only exclusion from the gift tax is the annual per donee exclusion of $3,000, or $6,000 in the case of gift-splitting by spouses (Code § 2503(b)). Any transfer by gift from one person to or for the benefit of another for the payment of tuition or medical services was not given any special treatment but was covered by the general annual per donee exclusion (other than special rules for gifts between spouses).[12]

### (d)    Reason for Change

Congress decided to create an additional tax incentive for the payment of a person's educational or medical expenses by another.

### (e)    Specifics of Law Revision

In addition to the increase in the general annual per donee exclusion to $10,000,[13] a new rule (Code § 2503(e)) allows an unlimited gift tax exclusion in two circumstances. One is for the payment of an amount on behalf of another individual as tuition to an educational organization (Code § 170(b)(i)(A)(ii)) for the education or training of the individual. (Thus, this transfer must, to qualify for the exclusion, be made directly to the educational institution, rather than to the student.) The other is for the payment of an amount on behalf of another individual to

[12]See Chapter 4 § 2.
[13]*Ibid.*

any person who provides medical care (Code § 213(e)) with respect to the individual for the medical care.

This provision will undoubtedly result in payments to universities, colleges, schools, hospitals, and the like that would otherwise not be received or at least not received on a timely basis.

## § 3.10   Extension of Prohibition on Fringe Benefit Regulations

(a)   Summary of Law Revision

The Department of the Treasury is prohibited from issuing final regulations relating to the income tax treatment of fringe benefits (Act § 801).

(b)   Effective Date

The prohibition on fringe benefit regulations is effective as of June 1, 1981.

(c)   Prior Law

Code § 61 defines gross income as including "all income from whatever source derived" and specifically refers to "compensation for services." The law is clear that "income" includes "compensation for services" paid for in a form other than money. A United States Supreme Court opinion states that Code § 61 is "broad enough to include in taxable income any economic or financial benefit conferred on the employee as compensation whatever the form or make by which it is effected." However, this so-called economic benefit test has not been rigidly followed in actual practice. Where compensation has been paid in a form other than cash, the tax treatment of the compensation has been determined by various statutes, regulations, and administrative rulings which take account of several factors.

In 1975, the Department of the Treasury issued a discussion draft of proposed regulations which contained rules for determining whether various fringe benefits constitute taxable compensation. These rules would have resulted in the taxation of certain employee fringe benefits that had not been taxed as a matter of prior administrative practice. Late in 1976, in the face of considerable controversy that had arisen in response to this proposal, the Treasury Department withdrew the discussion draft. Thus, the question of whether a particular fringe benefit is taxable compensation to employees generally continues to depend on the facts and circumstances of each case.

Because of this controversy and the uncertainty facing taxpayers on this subject, and inasmuch as Congress believed (and continues to believe) that any general taxation of fringe benefits should be subject to rules formulated by the legislative branch rather than by the executive branch, Congress acted in 1978 to prohibit the Department of the Treasury, prior to 1980, from issuing final regulations relating to the tax treatment of fringe benefits. This moratorium was subsequently extended through May 31, 1981.

Proposals made in recent years concerning guidelines for the tax treatment of employee fringe benefits include a package of recommendations from the Task Force on Employee Fringe Benefits of the House Committee on Ways and Means in the 95th Congress.

Most recently, the Treasury Department, during the Carter administration, submitted a discussion draft of proposed regulations on the subject to the House Ways and Means Committee.

(d)   Reason for Revision

Congress continues to believe that the basic rules concerning the federal income tax treatment of employee fringe benefits should be developed by it rather than by the Department of the Treasury and/or the Internal Revenue Service. Consequently, the purpose of the moratorium is to give Congress additional time to legislate on this complex and emotional subject.

(e)   Specifics of Law Revision

The prohibition on the issuance of final regulations concerning the federal income tax treatment of employee fringe benefits, previously imposed on the Department of the Treasury through May 31, 1981, is extended through December 31, 1983.

This moratorium thus stymies the general federal income taxation of fringe benefits received by employees, including the employees of nonprofit institutions and organizations. Potentially taxable is the value of such items as the provision of automobiles, parking, housing, club memberships, and travel. The rules ultimately formulated could affect analogous programs, such as the tuition remission programs administered by universities, colleges, and schools.

# 4

# The New Tax Rules Adversely Affecting Charitable Giving

## § 4.1 Introduction

The Act is being perceived by many as a pro-philanthropy tax law. This is largely because of such provisions as the charitable contribution deduction for individuals who do not itemize all deductions and the enlarged charitable contribution deduction for corporations.

In fact, however, the Act will likely do more to stymie and retard charitable giving than to stimulate it. This is because there are many provisions in the Act that will either reduce the tax incentive for giving or offer attractive alternative methods by which a person can transfer money or property for tax benefit. These provisions include the following: (1) a 23 percent across-the-board tax rate cut over 33 months, plus indexing of the rates and the like, for inflation (§ 2 hereof), (2) reduction of the top marginal individual income tax rate to 50 percent from 70 percent (§ 2), (3) repeal of the maximum tax in 1982 (§ 2), (4) reduction of the maximum capital gain tax rate for individuals to 20 percent from 28 percent (§ 3), (5) enactment of a 15

57

percent interest exclusion (§ 4), (6) enactment of a penalty for certain overstatements in the value of property that results in income tax underpayments (§ 5), (7) substantial liberalization of the estate and gift tax liabilities (§ 6), (8) expansion of the use of individual retirement accounts (§ 7), (9) creation of the so-called all savers certificates (§ 8), (10) increase in the exclusion of gain on the sale of a personal residence (§ 9), and (11) increase in the rollover period in connection with treatment of gain on the sale of a personal residence (§ 10).

## § 4.2   Individual Income Tax Reductions

It is a fundamental fact of tax life that an income tax deduction is worth more to taxpayers in the higher brackets than to those in the lower brackets. Thus, for example, a taxpayer who is in the 50 percent tax bracket and makes a charitable contribution economically experiences only a gift of one-half of the amount contributed and the federal government "subsidizes" the other half, while a taxpayer in the 20 percent tax bracket "pays" 80 percent of the gift and the government "subsidy" is only 20 percent. A corollary of this rule is that the income tax motivation for charitable giving is eroded to the extent tax rates decline.[1]

The individual income tax rates in effect prior to the Act begin at 14 percent on taxable income above $3,400 on a joint return and $2,400 on a single return. The rates range up to 70 percent on taxable incomes in excess of $215,400 on a joint return and $108,300 on a single return.

Thus, the highest marginal rate is 70 percent on taxable income in excess of $215,400 on a joint return and $108,300 on a single return. The top rate on personal service income is limited to 50 percent (the maximum tax). This rate applies above $60,000 on a joint return and $41,500 on a single return.

The Act (§ 101, Code §§ 1 and 6428) provides for cumulative

[1] There is no question that the independent sector is in a quandary in this regard, inasmuch as it cannot be in the position of championing higher tax rates and liabilities in the hope of making the charitable contribution deduction "worth more."

across-the-board income tax reductions for individuals of 23 percent by 1984 as follows:

| 1981 | 1.25 percent |
| 1982 | 10 |
| 1983 | 19 |
| 1984 | 23 |

Withholding tax changes take place on October 1, 1981 (5 percent), July 1, 1982 (10 percent), and July 1, 1983 (10 percent). Other withholding tax changes will cause the Treasury Department to issue regulations to enable employees to adjust their withholdings to more closely match their tax liability (Code § 3402(m)).

The new rules also provide some relief from the so-called marriage penalty by allowing a couple filing a joint return a deduction in computing adjusted gross income equal to a percentage of the lower-earning spouse's qualified earned income, up to a maximum of $30,000. In 1982, the percentage will be 5 percent (up to a $1,500 maximum deduction) and in 1983 and subsequent years the percentage will be 10 percent (up to a $3,000 maximum deduction) (Act § 103; Code § 221).

Also reduced are the top marginal tax rates from 70 percent to 50 percent in 1982. The maximum tax is scheduled for repeal in 1982, since there will no longer be a tax rate distinction between personal service income and unearned income (Act § 101(c)).

These individual income tax rate reductions will have the unavoidable consequence of eroding the tax motivation for charitable giving by reducing the "worth" of the charitable contribution deduction. However, inasmuch as the rate reductions are being phased in over four years, optimal tax planning dictates that deductions be utilized early and that income be deferred to the extent lawfully possible. For example, a taxpayer would likely be well advised to make charitable contributions or prepay charitable pledges to the extent possible in 1981 or 1982.

This erosion in the tax incentive for charitable giving is compounded by reason of the fact that the individual income tax rates are to be adjusted for inflation. At the present, the individual income tax is based upon various fixed amounts including the amounts that define the tax brackets, the zero bracket amount (the previous "standard deduction"), and the personal exemption. Under the Act, these items are to be adjusted for inflation (as measured by the Consumer Price Index), commencing in 1985 (Act § 104; Code §§ 1(f), 63(d), and 151(f)). If inflation persists in the coming years, the tax incentives for charitable giving will be further reduced.

## § 4.3    Individual Capital Gain Tax Rate Reductions

A deduction from gross income is allowed for 60 percent of any net capital gain for a tax year. That is, only 40 percent of a taxpayer's annual net capital gain is subject to federal income taxation. This 40 percent of net capital gain is taxed at the ordinary income tax rates up to 70 percent. Thus, the top effective tax rate on capital gains is 28 percent (the 70 percent rate times the 40 percent amount included in taxable income).

The Act (§ 102) reduced the top marginal income tax rate from 70 percent to 50 percent[2] in 1982. Correspondingly, the maximum effective tax rate on capital gain is lowered from 28 percent to 20 percent (the 50 percent rate times the 40 percent amount included in taxable income).

A special alternative tax for 1981 provides that a maximum 20 percent rate on net capital gain for individuals applies to sales or exchanges occurring after June 9, 1981. This provision does not apply to taxable receipts after June 9, 1981, of proceeds of sales or exchanges which occurred prior to that date.

As with any tax rate reduction, a lowering of the capital gain rates erodes the value of the charitable contribution deduction. This is particularly a problem for those organizations and institutions that rely substantially on major gifts from individuals. Many of these gifts—both outright and deferred—are funded with property that has appreciated in value. Two of the principal tax advantages to a donor of making a contribution to char-

[2]§ 4.2 hereof.

ity using appreciated property are that the charitable deduction is generally measured by the fair market value of the property (rather than the donor's cost basis in the property) and that any capital gain that would have been taxed had the property been sold or exchanged goes untaxed. However, as the capital gain tax rates are lowered, the "value" of the charitable contribution deduction in relation to the use of appreciated property is lessened.

Under existing law, an individual taxpayer can contribute appreciated property (such as stocks, bonds, and real estate), which if sold would give rise to long-term capital gain, to a public charity (essentially, a charitable organization other than a private foundation) and receive a charitable deduction for the full fair market value of the gift property, subject to an annual limitation of 30 percent of his or her adjusted gross income. (Outright cash gifts, for example, are limited by an annual ceiling of 50 percent.) Thus, the value of the deduction is the taxpayer's "basis" in the gift property (the original cost plus any capital improvements and sales costs) plus the entirety of the appreciation—and the appreciation element is not subjected to capital gains taxation. The appreciated property gift is, of course, utilized most by high-income taxpayers who, as noted, are a key source of financial support for educational, health, and other major institutions.

## § 4.4   Interest Exclusion

One of the chief tax advantages of a contribution to charity is, of course, that a taxpayer can transfer money or property to charity and receive a tax deduction in return. But in recent years, Congress has—largely to stimulate savings—created ways in which a taxpayer can transfer money or property in exchange for a tax benefit (deduction or exclusion) but where the taxpayer is also the beneficiary of the money or property transferred and the earnings thereon.

Under present law, individuals may exclude from income up to $200 ($400 on a joint return) of dividends and interest earned from most domestic sources in 1981 and 1982. After 1982, only the dividend exclusion, limited to $100 of dividends per taxpayer, was scheduled to be available. (This is the same dividend exclusion which applied before 1981.)

The Act (§ 302) repeals the $200/$400 interest and dividend exclusions after 1981 and institutes a $100 per taxpayer ($200 on a joint return) dividend exclusion for 1982 and subsequent years.

Effective in 1985, the law (Code § 128) will allow a 15 percent net interest (Code § 116(c)) exclusion up to $3,000 of net interest ($6,000 on a joint return). A qualified interest expense is interest paid for which a deduction is allowed, other than interest paid on debt related to a taxpayer's dwelling or his or her conduct of a trade or business. Also, only qualified interest expenses that give rise to a tax benefit are to reduce the amount of excludable interest, so an individual who does not itemize deductions will not be able to reduce excludable interest.

Thus, an individual acting solely with tax motivations in mind will have to assess the relative value of two "competing" transactions: (1) a charitable contribution with the resulting charitable deduction or (2) an investment that gives rise to excludable interest. Note that in the latter alternative, the taxpayer also retains the amount of principal transferred.

## § 4.5   Penalty for Certain Overstatements of Value

Congress decided to make the penalties for the overvaluation of property for tax purposes more stringent.

The law prior to the Act (Code § 6653) imposes an addition to tax, or penalty, with respect to certain tax underpayments due to negligence or civil fraud. The penalty for negligence is 5 percent of any underpayment that is due to negligent or intentional disregard for rules and regulations but not with intent to defraud.[3] The alternative civil fraud penalty is 50 percent of any underpayment.

[3]The Act (§ 722) imposes, in addition to the negligence penalty, a (nondeductible) tax equal to 50 percent of the interest (Code § 6601) attributable to that portion of an underpayment which is attributable to negligent or intentional disregard of rules or regulations (Code § 6653(a)).

The Act (§ 722) provides for a graduated addition to tax applicable to certain income tax "valuation overstatements" (Code § 6659). This addition to tax applies only to the extent of any income tax underpayment which is attributable to a valuation overstatement and only if the taxpayer is an individual, a closely held corporation (Code § 465(a)(1)(C)), or a personal service corporation (Code § 414(m)(3)).

A valuation overstatement occurs if the value of any property, or the adjusted basis of any property, claimed on any tax return exceeds 150 percent of the amount determined to be the correct amount of the valuation, or adjusted basis. If there is a valuation overstatement, the following percentages are to be used to determine the applicable addition to tax:

| If the valuation claimed is the following percent of the correct valuation | The applicable percentage is |
| --- | --- |
| 150 percent or more but not more than 200 percent | 10 |
| more than 200 percent but not more than 250 percent | 20 |
| more than 250 percent | 30[4] |

[4]There are two exceptions to the new penalty. First, the valuation overstatement penalty does not apply if the underpayment for the tax year attributable to the valuation overstatement is less than $1,000. Under this exception, the penalty could apply to one or more, but less than all, tax years affected by the valuation overstatement. Second, the penalty is inapplicable to any property which, as of the close of the tax year for which there is a valuation overstatement, has been held by the taxpayer for more than five years. In addition, the bill grants the tax authorities discretionary authority to waive all or part of the penalty on a showing by the taxpayer that there was a reasonable basis for the valuation or adjusted basis claimed on the return and that the claim was made in good faith.

While this penalty will apply in all income tax contexts, it will be applicable to reductions in tax liability by reason of charitable deductions based on the value of property. Thus, donors will have to keep this rule in mind when valuing such hard-to-value gift items as closely held stock and works of art. These rules will also apply to the calculation of a taxpayer's basis in property. So, for example, in determining the tax treatment of a gift of appreciated property, both the ascertainment of basis and of current value are potentially subject to this new penalty.

## § 4.6    Revision in General Estate and Gift Tax Rules

By reason of enactment of the Act, the unified credit against estate and gift taxes is gradually increased, the maximum gift and estate tax rates are reduced, the estate and gift tax marital deductions are liberalized, the "current use" valuation rules for qualified real property in estates are liberalized, the transfer-in-contemplation-of-death rule is generally repealed, the rules concerning the time for payment of estate tax attributable to closely held businesses are revised, the generation-skipping transfer tax transition rule is extended, the annual gift tax exclusion is increased, and the time for filing gift tax returns is changed (Act §§ 401, 402, 403, 421, 423, 424, 425, 428, 429, 441, and 442).

The new unified credit against estate and gift taxes is phased in between 1982 and 1987.

The new gift and estate tax rates are reduced over the period 1982–1985.

The new estate and gift tax marital deduction rules become effective for deaths and gifts after December 31, 1981.

The changes to the current use valuation provision apply generally to the estates of decedents dying after December 31, 1981. However, the increase in the limitation on the amount by which the fair market value of specially valued property can be reduced applies to estates of decedents dying after December 31, 1980.

The revised predeath qualified use requirement is retroactive to estates of certain decedents dying after December 31, 1976.

The rule providing a two-year grace period during which the

postdeath qualified use requirement need not be met is retroactive to estates of certain decedents dying after December 31, 1976.

The rule concerning the qualification of property purchased from a decedent's estate is retroactive to the estates of certain decedents dying after December 31, 1976.

The general repeal of the rule concerning gifts by a decedent within three years of death is applicable to decedents dying after December 31, 1981.

One of the principal components of the Tax Reform Act of 1976 was its revamping of the federal estate and gift tax rules. Among the chief reforms in this regard was unification of the estate and gift taxes (Code §§ 2010 and 2515).

Thus, the previous general exemptions from these taxes ($60,000 estate tax exemption and $30,000 gift tax exemption) were repealed and a unified credit was substituted. The unified credits against estate and gift taxes were phased in as follows:

| Date of death or gift | Credit | Exemption equivalent[5] |
|---|---|---|
| 1977 | $30,000 | $120,666 |
| 1978 | 34,000 | 134,000 |
| 1979 | 38,000 | 147,333 |
| 1980 | 42,500 | 161,563 |
| 1981 and after | 47,000 | 175,625 |

The unified rates (Code § 2001) generally resulted in small increases in the previous estate tax rates but significantly increased the gift tax rates. The maximum tax rate was set at 70 percent.

The 1976 revisions liberalized the estate tax marital deduc-

[5]These figures are used to express the "value" of the credits in relation to what they mean in dollar equivalents if the old exemptions were involved.

tion, increasing it to cover transfers to a surviving spouse up to the greater of 50 percent of the adjusted gross estate or $250,000 (Code § 2056). The gift tax marital deduction was likewise increased, to shelter the first $100,000 of gifts to a spouse and 50 percent of gifts to a spouse in excess of $200,000 (Code § 2523).

Enactment of the estate tax revisions in 1976 included a special valuation concept for the family farm or business, designed to eliminate or reduce forced sales of such properties by the heirs in order to pay the estate taxes. In this context, qualified property need not be valued at its fair market value or "highest and best use" value but can be valued on the basis of its special use as a farm or business (Code § 2032A). (Fair market valuation would take into account any other uses for which the property might be utilized—most likely, other uses of the real estate involved.) Consequently, estates of equal size may be taxed at different rates because of the type or use of the property or properties comprising the taxable estate.

The fair market value of qualified real property may not be reduced by more than $500,000 as a result of current use valuation (Code § 2032A(a)(2)).

To receive special valuation, real property must be used or held for use as a farm or closely held business (a "qualified use") for five of the previous eight years before the decedent's death and on the date of death (Code § 2032A(b)(1)). The decedent or a member of his or her family must materially participate in the farm (or other business operation) for periods aggregating five years of the eight years before the decedent's death. However, if the decedent materially participates in the farm operation, any income derived from the farm is treated as earned income for social security purposes and, therefore, may reduce social security benefits.

An election to specially value qualified real property must be made on a timely filed estate tax return.

Farm real property may be specially valued using a formula valuation method. Under the formula method, the value of qualified real property is determined by (1) subtracting the average annual state and local real estate taxes for tracts of comparable land used for farming from the average annual gross cash rental for the tracts of comparable land and (2) dividing that amount by the average annual effective interest rate for all new federal land bank loans. Each average annual computation is made on the basis of the five most recent calendar years ending before the decedent's death (Code § 2032A(e)(7)).

If, within 15 years after the death of the decedent (and before the death of the qualified heir), specially valued property is disposed of to nonfamily members or ceases to be used for the farming or other closely held business purpose upon which basis it was valued in the decedent's estate, all or a portion of the federal estate tax benefits obtained by virtue of the reduced valuation are recaptured by means of a special "additional estate tax" or "recapture tax" imposed on the qualified heir. Failure by the heir or a member of the heir's family to materially participate in the business operation for periods aggregating three years or more during any eight-year period ending within 15 years after the decedent's death is treated as a cessation of the qualified use.

If an election is made to value property based on its current use, the qualified heir's income tax basis in the property is its current use value. No adjustment is made to this basis if the recapture tax is imposed (Code § 1016(c)).

Only property which is acquired from a decedent is eligible for current use valuation.

Likewise, only real property that passes to qualified heirs is eligible for current use valuation. The term "qualified heir" means a member of the decedent's family, including his or her spouse, lineal descendants, parents, grandparents, and aunts or uncles of the decedent and their descendants. The term does not include members of a spouse's family (Code § 2032A(e)(2)).

Also, the predeath qualified use and material participation requirement may be satisfied by the decedent or a member of the decedent's family. Likewise, the postdeath material participation requirement may be satisfied by participation of the qualified heir or a member of the heir's family. Property can be disposed of during the recapture period without imposition of a recapture tax only if the transfer is to a member of the qualified heir's family.

Only real property used for farming purposes or in other closely held business operations (a "qualified use") is eligible for current use valuation. Timber operations are included in the definition of farming purposes. Standing timber, like other growing crops, is not treated as part of the qualified real property.

Generally, gifts made by a decedent within three years of death must be included in the decedent's gross estate at their value as of the date of death or alternate valuation date (Code § 2035(a)).

The rules enacted in 1976 include a tax on generation-skipping transfers (Code §§ 2601–2603 and 2611–2614). A transitional rule exempts from the tax generation-skipping trusts created by wills or revocable trusts in existence on June 11, 1976, if (1) such wills and trusts were not amended after that date to create a, or increase the amount of the, generation-skipping transfer and (2) the testator or trust grantor dies before January 1, 1982.

The annual per donee gift tax exclusion is $3,000 (Code § 2503(b)). Gift-splitting may increase the exclusion to $6,000.

Gift tax returns must be filed, and any gift tax paid, on a quarterly basis if the sum of (1) the taxable gifts made during the quarter and (2) all other taxable gifts made during the tax year (for which a return has not yet been required to be filed) exceed $25,000. If annual gifts are less than $25,000, a return must be filed for the fourth quarter (Code §§ 1015, 2501, 2502, 2503(a), 2504(a), 2505, 2512, 2513, 2522, 6019, 6075(b)).

Congress decided to relieve a variety of estate and gift tax liabilities, and to generally significantly reduce the number of estates subject to federal taxation.

The unified credit against estate and gift taxes is gradually increased from $47,000 to $192,800 over six years, as follows:

| Date of death or gift | Credit | Exemption equivalent |
|---|---|---|
| 1982 | $62,800 | $225,000 |
| 1983 | 79,300 | 275,000 |
| 1984 | 96,300 | 325,000 |
| 1985 | 121,800 | 400,000 |
| 1986 | 155,800 | 500,000 |
| 1987 and after | 192,800 | 600,000 |

The maximum gift and estate tax rates are reduced over a four-year period in 5 percent increments from 70 percent to 50 percent. The maximum rate is 65 percent for gifts made and decedents dying in 1982, 60 percent in 1983, 55 percent in 1984, and 50 percent in 1985 and subsequent years. When fully phased in, in 1985, the 50 percent tax rate will apply to taxable gifts and bequests in excess of $2.5 million.

The Act removes the quantitative limits on both the gift and estate tax marital deductions. Thus, these deductions are now unlimited deductions.

Concerning the increase in the maximum reduction in the amount of the fair market value of qualified real property pursuant to the current use valuation rules, the maximum amounts are increased to $600,000 for estates of decedents dying in 1981, $700,000 in 1982, and $750,000 in 1983 and thereafter.

As to the predeath qualified use requirement, it is now satisfied if either the decedent or a member of the decedent's family uses real property otherwise eligible for current use valuation in the qualified use (Code § 2032A(b)(1)).

As to the predeath material participation requirement, it now has to be satisfied during periods aggregating five years or more of the eight-year period ending before the earlier of (1) the date of death, (2) the date on which the decedent became disabled (which condition lasted until the date of the decedent's death), or (3) the date on which the individual began receiving social security retirement benefits (which status continued until the date of the decedent's death). An individual is considered to be disabled if the individual is mentally or physically unable to materially participate in the operation of the farm or other business.

The Act also creates an alternative to the material participation requirement for qualification of real property for current use valuation in the estates of surviving spouses who receive the property from a decedent spouse in whose estate it was eligible to be valued based on its current use. The new rule provides that the spouse will be treated as having materially participated during periods when the spouse (but not a family member) engaged in active management of the farm or other business operation. Active management means the making of business decisions other than the daily operating decisions of a farm or other trade or business.

Concerning the election requirements, an election to specially value property now must be made on the decedent's estate tax return rather than by the due date of the return. Therefore, the election is permitted to be made on a late return, if that return is the first estate tax return filed by the estate. (As under prior law, the election is irrevocable once made.)

A new rule permits substitution of net share rentals for cash rentals in the formula valuation method for farm real property if the executor cannot identify actual tracts of comparable farm real property in the same locality as the decedent's farm property that are rented solely for cash (Code § 2032A(e)(7)(B)). (As under prior law, if there is no comparable land from which a cash (or share) rental can be determined, the real property subject to the election is to be valued using the so-called multiple factor valuation method.)

As to the postdeath recapture period, the Act reduces the 15-year recapture period to 10 years. (The five-year phase-out period under prior law was repealed.)

Concerning the basis of property on which a recapture tax must be paid, the new rules permit a qualified heir to make an irrevocable election to have the income tax basis of qualified real property increased to the fair market value of the property as of the date of the decedent's death (or the alternate valuation date of Code § 2032, if the estate elected that provision) where the recapture tax is paid (Code § 1016(c)). If the heir elects this adjustment in basis, the heir must pay interest on the amount of the recapture tax from the period which begins nine months after the decedent's death and concludes with the due date of the recapture tax. The interest is computed at the rate or rates charged on deficiencies of tax for the period involved. If the heir does not make the election and pay the interest, no adjustment is made to the basis of the property.

In amplification of the requirement that a qualified heir owning the real property after the decedent's death must use it in the qualified use throughout the recapture period, a new rule creates a special two-year grace period immediately following the date of the decedent's death during which failure by the qualified heir to commence use of the property in the qualified use will not result in imposition of a recapture tax. The 10-year recapture period discussed above (15 years for estates of decedents dying before December 31, 1981) is extended by a period equal to any part of the two-year grace period which expires before the qualified heir commences using the property in the qualified use (Code § 2032A(c)(7)).

In the case of an eligible qualified heir, a new rule provides that "active management" by the eligible qualified heir is treated as material participation for purposes of meeting the material participation requirement during the postdeath recapture periods. Eligible qualified heirs include the spouse of the decedent, a qualified heir who has not attained the age of 21, a qualified heir who is a full-time student (Code § 151(e)(4)), and a qualified heir who is disabled (within the meaning of newly enacted Code § 2032A(b)(4)(B)). "Active management" means the making of business decisions other than the daily operating decisions of the trade or business.

An exchange (pursuant to Code § 1031) of qualified real property solely for qualified replacement property to be used for the same qualified use as the original qualified real property does not result in imposition of the recapture tax.

The requirement that a qualified heir make an election to secure the benefits of the special nonrecognition rules for the recapture tax for involuntary conversions has been repealed.

A new rule expands the circumstances in which property is considered acquired from a decedent, for purposes of current use valuation, to include property that is purchased from a decedent's estate by a qualified heir, as well as property that is received by bequest, devise, inheritance, or in satisfaction of a right to pecuniary bequest. This change reverses prior law in cases where the decedent gives a qualified heir an option to purchase property otherwise qualified for current use valuation as well as in cases where the executor or executrix sells the property to an heir in the absence of such a direction in the will. If purchased property is specially valued, the qualified heir who purchases the property is limited to the current use value of the property as his or her income tax basis.

For purposes of the current use valuation rules, the definition of the term "family member" has been changed. The new definition includes an individual's spouse, parents, brothers and sisters, children, stepchildren, and spouses and lineal descendants of these individuals (Code § 2032A(e)(2)).

As to the rules for woodlands, the law continues the treatment of timber operations as a farming use but permits executors to elect to specially value the standing timber. If standing timber is specially valued, the recapture tax is imposed when the timber is disposed of or severed (Code §§ 2032A(e)(13), 2032A(c)(2)).

In general, the Act repeals the estate tax rule concerning transfers within three years of death (Code § 2035(d)(1)). However, prior law continues to apply to gifts of certain types of property (Code §§ 2036, 2037, 2038, 2041, and 2042). Also, all gifts made within three years of death are included in estates for purposes of qualifying for current use valuation (Code § 2032A), deferred payment of estate tax (Code § 6166), qualified redemptions to pay estate tax (Code § 303), and estate tax liens (chapter 64, subchapter C) (Code § 2035(d)(2)).

The basis of appreciated property acquired by gift within one year of death is not adjusted to its fair market value at date of death if it is returned to the donor or the donor's spouse (Code § 1014(e)).

The generation-skipping transfer tax transitional rule is extended an additional year, to January 1, 1983.

The amount of the annual gift tax exclusion is increased from $3,000 to $10,000 per donee.

All gift tax returns are to be filed, and any gift tax paid, on an annual basis.

The foregoing revisions of the estate and gift tax rules will likely dampen the prospects for charitable giving through decedent's estates. For example, the number of estates being taxed at all is being sharply reduced so that the utility of the charitable deduction in this context is being reduced as well. Also, the estate and gift tax charitable deductions are being eroded by reason of such law changes as the lowering of the maximum estate and gift tax rates, the considerable liberalization of the estate and gift tax marital deductions, and the expansion of the annual per donee gift tax exclusion. Further, the rules concerning estate tax valuation of family farm property and closely held businesses are being relaxed, thereby lessening the likelihood that such properties will be the subject of transfers to charity.

## § 4.7   Individual Retirement Account Rules Expansion

The Act (§ 311) importantly expands the utilization of individual retirement accounts. In so doing, the Act creates another alternative to charitable giving for the tax-motivated donor:[6] (1) should he or she contribute to charity and enjoy the resulting charitable deduction or (2) should he or she contribute to a fund to benefit himself or herself by means of retirement benefits and enjoy the resulting deduction? The advantages of the second alternative are compounded by reason of the fact that the deduction achieved because of a qualified contribution to an individual retirement account is an "above-the-line" deduction[7] (that is, used in computing adjusted gross income rather than taxable income) that may be taken by a taxpayer irrespective of whether deductions are itemized, and that the earnings on the amount transferred also return to the taxpayer without taxation until retirement.

Under the law in effect for tax years beginning before December 31, 1981, an individual who is not an active participant in an employer-sponsored retirement plan can deduct contributions to an individual retirement account up to the lesser of $1,500 or 15 percent of compensation. The ceiling is $1,750 for contributions to an individual retirement account equally divided between an individual and his or her nonworking spouse (the "spousal" individual retirement account).

The law created by the Act (Code § 219) raises the annual contribution limit to an individual retirement account, in the case of an individual who is not an active participant in an employer-sponsored plan, to the lesser of $2,000 or 100 percent

[6]See § 4 hereof.
[7]See Chapter 2 § 2.

of compensation. The limit for a spousal individual retirement account is increased to $2,250 and the requirement that contributions under a spousal individual retirement account be equally divided between the spouses is repealed.

As noted, under prior law, an active participant in an employer-sponsored qualified retirement plan cannot deduct contributions made to an individual retirement account. However, the new law allows such an employee a deduction for contributions to an individual retirement account.[8] These contributions are subject to the dollar limitations of the individual retirement account rules.

## § 4.8    All Savers Certificates

The Act, in providing special tax treatment for the new, so-called all savers certificates, establishes yet another alternative for the tax-oriented taxpayer to the charitable deduction.[9] Here, the choice is much like that to be accorded by the forthcoming interest exclusion,[10] namely, will a taxpayer decide to make a charitable contribution and have the benefit of the resulting charitable deduction or will the taxpayer instead "contribute" money or property to an eligible institution and take the tax benefits in the form of excludable interest (all the while retaining access to the principal transferred)?

As noted,[11] the only exclusion under the law antedating the Act for interest income is the special provision for 1981 and 1982 sheltering up to $200 ($400 on a joint return) of dividends and interest from a variety of domestic sources (Code § 116).

A new rule instituted by enactment of the Act (§ 301) provides for a lifetime exclusion from gross income of $1,000

---

[8]A separate newly enacted rule now allows a deduction for an employee who makes a voluntary contribution to a qualified employer retirement plan, with the contributions subject to the basic dollar limitations of the individual retirement account rules (Act § 311; Code § 219).

[9]See § 4 hereof.

[10]*Ibid.*

[11]*Ibid.*

($2,000 in the case of a joint return) of interest earned on these qualified savings certificates (Code § 128).

Qualified certificates are one-year certificates issued after September 30, 1981, and before January 1, 1983, by a qualified depository institution. Such a certificate must have a yield equal to 70 percent of the yield on 52-week Treasury bills. A qualified depository institution is a bank, a mutual savings bank, cooperative bank, domestic building and loan association, industrial loan association or bank, credit union, or any other savings or thrift institution chartered and supervised under federal or state law, if the deposits or accounts of the institution (other than an industrial loan association) are insured under federal or state law or protected or guaranteed by state law.

Generally, at least 75 percent of the proceeds of qualified certificates issued during a calendar quarter by an institution (other than a credit union) must be used to provide residential financing by the end of the subsequent calendar quarter.

## § 4.9   Increase in Gain Exclusion Upon Sale of Residence

An important feature of the federal income tax laws in relation to tax incentives for charitable giving is that a taxpayer, faced with a burden of retaining ownership of property, can almost always relieve himself or herself of that burden by contributing the property to charity, and usually receive a useful deduction as well. In the case of real property, such a burden might be the payment of real estate taxes or a substantial capital gain tax. This form of relief can be provided by an outright gift to charity or a deferred gift to charity.

However, to the extent Congress directly reduces the extent of that burden, this incentive for charitable giving is likewise reduced.[12]

This result is occurring with respect to the capital gain tax

[12]An example of this principle (other than that of this section and § 10) is the easing of the rules by which family farms and/or closely held businesses may have to be sold by heirs or contributed to charity because of the estate tax liability (§ 6 hereof).

liability facing taxpayers who reach a point in their lives where the personal residence must be sold. Such a liability may stimulate a taxpayer to make a contribution of the residence to charity.

Present law provides some relief in this regard by allowing individuals who have attained the age of 55 to elect a one-time exclusion of up to $100,000 of gain on the sale of their personal residence (Code § 121). Generally, the individual must have owned and used the property as a principal residence for three years or more out of the five-year period preceding the sale.

In a revision of this law that will further depress the tax incentive for contributions of personal residences, the Act (§ 123) increased to $125,000 the amount of gain excludable from gross income on the sale or exchange of a principal residence by an individual who has attained the age of 55. This new rule is effective for sales and exchanges of a principal residence after July 20, 1981.

### § 4.10   Increase in Rollover Period Following Sale of Residence

The same fact of tax life discussed in the preceding section was also affected by another revision in the tax rules concerning the disposition of a personal residence.

Present law provides for the deferral of the recognition, or rollover, of gain on the sale of a taxpayer's principal residence if a new principal residence is purchased and used by the taxpayer within a period beginning 18 months before and ending 18 months after, the sale (Code § 1034). This rule applies only to the extent that the purchase price of the replacement residence equals or exceeds the sale price of the residence sold.

The Act (§ 122) extended the 18-month replacement period of this rule to two years. This change is effective for sales and exchanges of principal residences after July 20, 1981, and for such sales and exchanges with respect to which the 18-month rollover period has not expired on or before July 20, 1981. It is not effective for sales and exchanges of principal residences for which the 18-month rollover period has expired by July 21, 1981.

# 5

# The 1981 Tax Act: A Look Ahead

A principal hallmark of the Reagan Administration thus far is proposed budget cuts in more than 80 programs—specifically, $133.9 billion over fiscal years 1981, 1982, and 1983. This slashing of the budget, coupled with the just-enacted tax revisions, is being hailed as the most dramatic reshuffling of economic priorities in this country since institution of the government programs that led to recovery from the Depression.

In evaluating these economic policies as they relate to non-profit organizations, it is tempting to fall into the typical pattern of lamenting those cuts that land close to home. Nonprofit organizations that rely heavily on federal funding are among those protesting the proposed reductions in federal economic assistance. They will be directly affected by cuts of $4.8 billion set for fiscal year 1981 and $48.6 billion for fiscal year 1982.

The range of federal undertakings that the Administration wishes to eliminate or reduce is indeed staggering. The threatened programs include those in the areas of welfare, health care, public jobs and training, space, food stamps, the arts, education, mass transit, foreign aid, consumer protection, water projects, synthetic fuels, legal services, milk price supports, and a variety of benefits programs, such as those for veterans and unemployment insurance. It is estimated that cuts in programs which primarily aid the poor will total over $16 billion in fiscal year 1982.

However, the longer-range view concerning these budget cuts (assuming they are implemented) may be that the new economic policies will provide an enormous opportunity for nonprofit organizations.

The reason for this opportunity can be found in the basic rationale for nonprofit organizations in American society. This rationale takes root in our political philosophy which stresses individual initiative and institutional pluralism. The rationale holds that not all decision making and problem solving is to repose in government. Ample room exists for individuals to improve their society by working through a system of organizations other than governmental ones. Therefore, the existence and proliferation of nonprofit groups (particularly the charitable ones) afford individuals the means to channel their interests and energies toward the resolution of societal problems.

This reliance on a range of nonprofit organizations—today known as the "independent sector"—is supposed to distinguish the United States from other nations. In other countries, those contemplating the solution to a problem will instinctively turn to government for help. Here, the difference is that we are thought to be more self-reliant, more likely to band together to attack the problem collectively, and perhaps even distrust the government.

However true this may have been historically, it cannot be disputed that in recent years the country has deviated from this pattern. The years of the Great Society epitomized the entry of government into new realms—domains once solely those of individual initiative and activity. The government thus began providing services on a substantial level in the fields of the arts, education, health care, aid to the elderly, assistance to the poor, and the like. Not only were these areas previously the provinces of the nonprofit community, but this shift in emphasis on involvement of government also caused many nonprofit organizations to become heavily reliant on funding from government. Concurrent with the expansion of government has come the atrophy of the independent sector. (As the nation expands, so does the nonprofit community. Its growth, however, has been curbed by the concomitant expansion of government.)

Therefore, if government is now to shrink, logic dictates that the independent sector take up at least some of the slack. The services that were once provided by government in the various domains of service programs can now be provided by nonprofit organizations. Such important functions as fighting poverty, promoting the arts, and expanding access to education could be restored to the nonprofit world where they once were. Not only would this ensure continuity of the services, it would also be fully compatible with traditional American political philosophy and the rationale for nonprofit organizations.

In fact, it is surprising that the Reagan Administration, in its zeal to curb the expansion of government and balance the budget, does not endeavor to temper the criticism of those who label it callous for terminating government-provided or -sponsored services by calling on the independent sector to step in and claim its rightful role of providing these needed functions.

The instant response to all of the foregoing must be the question as to where the independent sector is going to find the support to provide these services, involving billions of dollars, in lieu of the federal government. This is a particularly pressing question for those nonprofits that have become dependent upon federal funding.

This difficulty is compounded by reason of the fact that the Act, across several fronts, erodes tax incentives for giving to charitable organizations. While, as noted, this outcome was not a deliberate objective of the Act, it is ironic that the Reagan Administration budget cuts—which are cutting off funding to nonprofit organizations while simultaneously increasing the need for their services—are being promptly followed by tax revisions that will dampen donors' propensities to provide the very support that these organizations will so desperately require.

There are a variety of answers to the question as to where the independent sector agencies will locate needed gift dollars. Some of the answers involve new law changes, while other require utilization of existing opportunities.

First, nonprofit organizations must take a renewed look at

development and maximize their fund-raising potential. For example, organizations that rely chiefly on direct mail fund-raising must explore other methods to secure funds. A variety of organizations should launch planned giving programs. Organizations that are not themselves classified as "charitable," "educational," "religious," "scientific," and the like must endeavor to create and utilize related "charitable" organizations. Too many organizations are not experiencing their full fund-raising potential, and others are wrongfully not engaging in fund-raising at all. The rule that "necessity is the mother of invention" should apply in this context and force nonprofit organizations to develop ways to expand their access to private sources of support.

Second, the federal government should become directly involved with this dilemma facing the nonprofit sector and become part of the process to effect the necessary solutions. This does not mean the establishment of a new government agency, with the attendant bureaucracy, forms, and studies. But some signal from the White House and/or Congress that the federal government is aware of this problem, and is willing to assist in its rectification, is essential.

The third answer is that government regulators and the contributing public must come to understand the realities of fund-raising and shape their regulatory and donative policies accordingly. Nonprofit organizations are faced with the same expenses as for-profits, and the costs of fund-raising (particularly for new organizations) will continue to climb. The current emphasis on fund-raising costs is, in addition to distorting government regulation, preventing regulators and prospective donors from focusing on the material elements as to what constitutes a meritorious organization. A variety of stringent state laws, overzealous independent watchdog agencies, and some emerging federal regulation via the tax laws are combining to make fund-raising for charitable purposes a highly overregulated activity. The present pace of growing regulation may soon destroy the existing system of private philanthropy and thus largely preclude the independent sector from reclaiming its rightful position in relation to government.

A final solution is that the federal tax laws must be revised to accord donors the encouragement and the economic means to provide greater support to the independent sector. Not only would this provide the nonprofit sector with needed resources, but it would also afford supporters the additional benefit of being able to target the beneficiaries of their assistance. Among the various proposals to do this is the new rule created by the Act to allow the deduction for charitable contributions by donors who do not otherwise itemize deductions. This law change alone should infuse the nonprofit sector with needed additional billions of dollars, which undoubtedly will be expended more efficiently than by government.

There are other tax proposals which could help in this regard, including (1) increasing (if not eliminating) the percentage limitations on the amounts of charitable gifts by individuals that may be annually deducted, concerning both gifts of money and of property, (2) allowing a donor a period of time into a year to make charitable gifts that would be deductible in ascertaining tax liability for the immediately preceding year, to facilitate planning and optimum use of the charitable contribution deduction, (3) creation of a means by which technically nonqualifying charitable remainder trusts can be reformed so as to allow the intended charitable deduction, (4) enactment of a deduction for artists for contributions of their works to charity, over the cost of materials as under present law, (5) elimination of the charitable deduction as an item to be considered in calculating taxable income subject to the alternative minimum tax, and (6) elimination of the rule requiring a reduction in the charitable deduction for the gift of an item of tangible personal property (such as artwork) where the property will not or cannot be directly used by the recipient organization in exempt purposes.

There is already talk of a new tax bill. (During consideration of the Act, the Congressional leadership continuously held out the prospect of a second tax bill during this Congress, to forestall amendments to the Act, but the promise was not regarded seriously.) Another tax act within the coming months would provide an opportunity to build into federal law additional tax motivations for charitable giving. Recognition of the worth and role of the nonprofit sector in this fashion could be another substantial achievement for the Reagan Administration, and it would serve to offset some of the deterrents to tax-motivated charitable giving introduced by the Act.

Another tax measure would accord the Reagan Administration the opportunity to demonstrate its belief in the principle that the political and economic philosophy upon which this nation was founded and presumably remains organized strongly emphasizes individual initiative and the combatting of problems, the reaching of solutions, and the advancement of public ends by the voluntary sector of society. This is the principle of "pluralism," which stresses the inherent value of decentralized and nongovernmental choice-making and action as being essential to the preservation of individual liberty, as well as a system more responsive to public needs and more efficient than the cumbersome and less flexible allocation process of government administration. These doctrines have been articulated by many philosophers, including Alexis de Tocqueville and John Stuart Mill, and permeate the thinking of this country's founders, as evidenced, for example, in the Federalist Papers.

As de Tocqueville stated in his classic *Democracy in America,* when those in the private, voluntary sector in the United States embark on a public undertaking for the common good, they do so through "association." The widespread use of nonprofit organizations to advance public ends is unique to this country and is an integral feature of our traditions and societal structure. The role and responsibility of nonprofit entities in America is not diminished in modern society. Indeed, the need for the contributions of nonprofit organizations—whether in education, health, the arts, consumer and environmental protection, or whatever—is greater today than previously, particularly in view of the growing complexity and inefficiency of government.

Consequently, since the beginnings of the national income tax, charitable and other nonprofit groups have been exempted from the tax, and giving to qualified charitable organizations stimulated by the charitable contribution deduction. The latter tax provision accompanies the former because, of course, it is philanthropy that provides the resources that enables charitable groups to make their contributions to the country's progress. To construct a tax system any differently would be to flatly repudiate and contravene those doctrines which are so much a part of the nation's heritage.

Therefore, the federal tax exemption and deductions enacted to further charitable endeavors are not "loopholes," "preferences," or tax "subsidies." Congress has not "given" philanthropy any "benefits" but instead has legislated in recognition of these basic philosophical underpinnings. The charitable deduction (and exemption) thus is predicated on principles that are more fundamental than tax doctrines and are outside the Internal Revenue Code. The federal tax provisions enhancing charity exist as a reflection of the affirmative national policy of not inhibiting by taxation the beneficial activities of qualified organizations striving to advance the quality of the American social order.

Thus, the charitable contribution deduction is not an anachronism, a creature of a bygone era. Rather, it continues as a bulwark against overdomination by government and a hallmark of a free society; it helps nourish the voluntary sector of this nation and preserve individual initiative and reflects the pluralistic philosophy which has been the guiding spirit of democratic America. The charitable deduction has been proven to be fair and efficient, and without it the philanthropic sector of our society would be rendered unrecognizable by present standards.

Landrum R. Bolling, in 1975, in a pamphlet entitled "Philanthropy and the Private Sector in American Life," wrote that "the survival of this incredibly pluralistic society is tied to the broad use of volunteer institutions, activities, and programs to deal with a great variety of our needs and interests." Bolling, following a description of the "importance of encouraging voluntarism" and the "wisdom of decentralization," urged the development of a "comprehensive, coherent, and consistent public policy to encourage private philanthropy." Likewise, Gordon Manser, writing in 1977, observed: "What is of transcendent importance is recognition of the vital role of voluntary organizations in our society and willingness to shape and strengthen philanthropy so that its mission may be carried forward." To this same end, John D. Rockefeller III, in 1978, wrote that if the leadership of the government and business sectors of U.S. society were to assume the responsibility for support of the private sector, "[w]e would surprise ourselves and the world, because American democracy, which all too many observers believe is on a downward slide, would come alive with unimagined creativity and energy."

The utility of the charitable contribution deduction is deteriorating incrementally; its opponents are succeeding by chipping away at its foundation with the passage of each tax reform bill. Without a strong and affirmative defense, tax incentives for charitable giving may succumb some more again, this time at the hands of another Tax Reform Act. It is to be hoped that President and Congress will soon realize the folly of more tinkering in this area and will come to see the virtue of encouraging charitable giving instead of stymying it.

In sum, there needs to be a realization that the charitable deduction (and exemption) is predicated on principles that are more fundamental than tax doctrines and are larger than the technical considerations of the Internal Revenue Code. The federal tax provisions enhancing charity exist as a reflection of the affirmative national policy of not inhibiting by taxation the beneficial activities of qualified organizations striving to advance the quality of the American social order.

The Act, as noted, treats charitable organizations more fairly than have other tax revision proposals (enacted and not enacted) in the recent past. This may be a positive sign. Yet there is the unavoidable fact that the tailoring of the tax laws in furtherance of particular social policy can inadvertently damage the tax incentives for charitable giving.

That is why, with the services of the nonprofit sector back in full need, the federal tax laws need to be reconfigured to build in maximum reasonable motivation for support of the nation's independent sector. The Act tugs in both directions in this regard by simultaneously providing for some specific support for philanthropy while creating other law that will diminish such support.

The charitable sector must work to identify the tax law revisions that are most necessary to it and likewise identify the other tax law revisions (actual and proposed) that may prove most damaging to its support, and then devise and advance a legislative strategy with the objective of maximum tax support for philanthropy and maximum compatibility between charitable tax law rules and other tax law provisions. The next tax acts, and philanthropy's reaction and contribution to them, will—like the Act—say much about the role of philanthropy in the United States and the world in the coming years.

# APPENDICES

# Pertinent Provisions of the Economic Recovery Tax Act of 1981

## Table of Contents of Act*

(Section 1)

(a) SHORT TITLE.—This Act may be cited as the "Economic Recovery Tax Act of 1981".

(b) TABLE OF CONTENTS.—

*The sections of the Act followed by an asterisk are reproduced in this Appendix.

## TITLE II—BUSINESS INCENTIVE PROVISIONS

### Subtitle A—Cost Recovery Provisions

### Subtitle B—Investment Tax Credit Provisions

### Subtitle C—Incentives for Research and Experimentation

### Subtitle D—Small Business Provisions

(c) AMENDMENT OF 1954 CODE.—Except as otherwise expressly provided, whenever in this Act an amendment or repeal is expressed in terms of an amendment to, or repeal of, a section or other provision, the reference shall be considered to be made to a section or other provision of the Internal Revenue Code of 1954.

## Individual Income Tax Rate Reductions

(Section 101)

(a) RATE REDUCTION.—Section 1 (relating to tax imposed) is amended to read as follows:

"SECTION 1. TAX IMPOSED.

"(a) MARRIED INDIVIDUALS FILING JOINT RETURNS AND SURVIVING SPOUSES.—There is hereby imposed on the taxable income of every married individual (as defined in section 143) who makes a single return jointly with his spouse under section 6013, and every surviving spouse (as defined in section 2(a)), a tax determined in accordance with the following tables:

"(1) FOR TAXABLE YEARS BEGINNING IN 1982.—

| "If taxable income is: | The tax is: |
|---|---|
| Not over $3,400 | No tax. |
| Over $3,400 but not over $5,500 | 12% of the excess over $3,400. |
| Over $5,500 but not over $7,600 | $252, plus 14% of the excess over $5,500. |
| Over $7,600 but not over $11,900 | $546, plus 16% of the excess over $7,600. |
| Over $11,900 but not over $16,000 | $1,234, plus 19% of the excess over $11,900. |
| Over $16,000 but not over $20,200 | $2,013, plus 22% of the excess over $16,000. |
| Over $20,200 but not over $24,600 | $2,937, plus 25% of the excess over $20,200. |
| Over $24,600 but not over $29,900 | $4,037, plus 29% of the excess over $24,600. |
| Over $29,900 but not over $35,200 | $5,574, plus 33% of the excess over $29,900. |
| Over $35,200 but not over $45,800 | $7,323, plus 39% of the excess over $35,200. |
| Over $45,800 but not over $60,000 | $11,457, plus 44% of the excess over $45,800. |
| Over $60,000 but not over $85,600 | $17,705, plus 49% of the excess over $60,000. |
| Over $85,600 | $30,249, plus 50% of the excess over $85,600. |

"(2) FOR TAXABLE YEARS BEGINNING IN 1983.—

| "If taxable income is: | The tax is: |
|---|---|
| Not over $3,400 | No tax. |
| Over $3,400 but not over $5,500 | 11% of the excess over $3,400. |
| Over $5,500 but not over $7,600 | $231, plus 13% of the excess over $5,500. |

| "If taxable income is: | The tax is: |
|---|---|
| Over $7,600 but not over $11,900 ............... | $504, plus 15% of the excess over $7,600. |
| Over $11,900 but not over $16,000 ............. | $1,149, plus 17% of the excess over $11,900. |
| Over $16,000 but not over $20,200 ............. | $1,846, plus 19% of the excess over $16,000. |
| Over $20,200 but not over $24,600 ............. | $2,644, plus 23% of the excess over $20,200. |
| Over $24,600 but not over $29,900 ............. | $3,656, plus 26% of the excess over $24,600. |
| Over $29,900 but not over $35,200 ............. | $5,034, plus 30% of the excess over $29,900. |
| Over $35,200 but not over $45,800 ............. | $6,624, plus 35% of the excess over $35,200. |
| Over $45,800 but not over $60,000 ............. | $10,334, plus 40% of the excess over $45,800. |
| Over $60,000 but not over $85,600 ............. | $16,014, plus 44% of the excess over $60,000. |
| Over $85,600 but not over $109,400 .......... | $27,278, plus 48% of the excess over $85,600. |
| Over $109,400 ............................................. | $38,702, plus 50% of the excess over $109,400. |

## "(3) FOR TAXABLE YEARS BEGINNING AFTER 1983.—

| "If taxable income is: | The tax is: |
|---|---|
| Not over $3,400 ............................................ | No tax. |
| Over $3,400 but not over $5,500 ................. | 11% of the excess over $3,400. |
| Over $5,500 but not over $7,600 ................. | $231, plus 12% of the excess over $5,500. |
| Over $7,600 but not over $11,900 ............... | $483, plus 14% of the excess over $7,600. |
| Over $11,900 but not over $16,000 ............. | $1,085, plus 16% of the excess over $11,900. |
| Over $16,000 but not over $20,200 ............. | $1,741, plus 18% of the excess over $16,000. |
| Over $20,200 but not over $24,600 ............. | $2,497, plus 22% of the excess over $20,200. |
| Over $24,600 but not over $29,900 ............. | $3,465, plus 25% of the excess over $24,600. |
| Over $29,900 but not over $35,200 ............. | $4,790, plus 28% of the excess over $29,900. |
| Over $35,200 but not over $45,800 ............. | $6,274, plus 33% of the excess over $35,200. |
| Over $45,800 but not over $60,000 ............. | $9,772, plus 38% of the excess over $45,800. |
| Over $60,000 but not over $85,600 ............. | $15,168, plus 42% of the excess over $60,000. |
| Over $85,600 but not over $109,400 .......... | $25,920, plus 45% of the excess over $85,600. |
| Over $109,400 but not over $162,400 ......... | $36,630, plus 49% of the excess over $109,400. |
| Over $162,400 ............................................. | $62,600, plus 50% of the excess over $162,400. |

"(b) HEADS OF HOUSEHOLDS.—There is hereby imposed on the taxable income of every individual who is the head of a household (as defined in section 2(b)) a tax determined in accordance with the following tables:

"(1) FOR TAXABLE YEARS BEGINNING IN 1982.—

| "If taxable income is: | The tax is: |
|---|---|
| Not over $2,300 | No tax. |
| Over $2,300 but not over $4,400 | 12% of the excess over $2,300. |
| Over $4,400 but not over $6,500 | $252, plus 14% of the excess over $4,400. |
| Over $6,500 but not over $8,700 | $546, plus 16% of the excess over $6,500. |
| Over $8,700 but not over $11,800 | $898, plus 20% of the excess over $8,700. |
| Over $11,800 but not over $15,000 | $1,518, plus 22% of the excess over $11,800. |
| Over $15,000 but not over $18,200 | $2,222, plus 23% of the excess over $15,000. |
| Over $18,200 but not over $23,500 | $2,958, plus 28% of the excess over $18,200. |
| Over $23,500 but not over $28,800 | $4,442, plus 32% of the excess over $23,500. |
| Over $28,800 but not over $34,100 | $6,138, plus 38% of the excess over $28,800. |
| Over $34,100 but not over $44,700 | $8,152, plus 41% of the excess over $34,100. |
| Over $44,700 but not over $60,600 | $12,498, plus 49% of the excess over $44,700. |
| Over $60,600 | $20,289, plus 50% of the excess over $60,600. |

"(2) FOR TAXABLE YEARS BEGINNING IN 1983.—

| "If taxable income is: | The tax is: |
|---|---|
| Not over $2,300 | No tax. |
| Over $2,300 but not over $4,400 | 11% of the excess over $2,300. |
| Over $4,400 but not over $6,500 | $231, plus 13% of the excess over $4,400. |
| Over $6,500 but not over $8,700 | $504, plus 15% of the excess over $6,500. |
| Over $8,700 but not over $11,800 | $834, plus 18% of the excess over $8,700. |
| Over $11,800 but not over $15,000 | $1,392, plus 19% of the excess over $11,800. |
| Over $15,000 but not over $18,200 | $2,000, plus 21% of the excess over $15,000. |
| Over $18,200 but not over $23,500 | $2,672, plus 25% of the excess over $18,200. |
| Over $23,500 but not over $28,800 | $3,997, plus 29% of the excess over $23,500. |
| Over $28,800 but not over $34,100 | $5,534, plus 34% of the excess over $28,800. |
| Over $34,100 but not over $44,700 | $7,336, plus 37% of the excess over $34,100. |
| Over $44,700 but not over $60,600 | $11,258, plus 44% of the excess over $44,700. |
| Over $60,600 but not over $81,800 | $18,254, plus 48% of the excess over $60,600. |
| Over $81,800 | $28,430, plus 50% of the excess over $81,800. |

"(3) FOR TAXABLE YEARS BEGINNING AFTER 1983.—

| "If taxable income is: | The tax is: |
|---|---|
| Not over $2,300 | No tax. |
| Over $2,300 but not over $4,400 | 11% of the excess over $2,300. |

| "If taxable income is: | The tax is: |
|---|---|
| Over $4,400 but not over $6,500 ................ | $231, plus 12% of the excess over $4,400. |
| Over $6,500 but not over $8,700 ................ | $483, plus 14% of the excess over $6,500. |
| Over $8,700 but not over $11,800 .............. | $791, plus 17% of the excess over $8,700. |
| Over $11,800 but not over $15,000 ............ | $1,318, plus 18% of the excess over $11,800. |
| Over $15,000 but not over $18,200 ............ | $1,894, plus 20% of the excess over $15,000. |
| Over $18,200 but not over $23,500 ............ | $2,534, plus 24% of the excess over $18,200. |
| Over $23,500 but not over $28,800 ............ | $3,806, plus 28% of the excess over $23,500. |
| Over $28,800 but not over $34,100 ............ | $5,290, plus 32% of the excess over $28,800. |
| Over $34,100 but not over $44,700 ............ | $6,986, plus 35% of the excess over $34,100. |
| Over $44,700 but not over $60,600 ............ | $10,696, plus 42% of the excess over $44,700. |
| Over $60,600 but not over $81,800 ............ | $17,374, plus 45% of the excess over $60,600. |
| Over $81,800 but not over $108,300 .......... | $26,914, plus 48% of the excess over $81,800. |

"(c) UNMARRIED INDIVIDUALS (OTHER THAN SURVIVING SPOUSES AND HEADS OF HOUSEHOLDS).—There is hereby imposed on the taxable income of every individual (other than a surviving spouse as defined in section 2(a) or the head of a household as defined in section 2(b)) who is not a married individual (as defined in section 143) a tax determined in accordance with the following tables:

"(1) FOR TAXABLE YEARS BEGINNING IN 1982.—

| "If taxable income is: | The tax is: |
|---|---|
| Not over $2,300 ............................................. | No tax. |
| Over $2,300 but not over $3,400 ................ | 12% of the excess over $2,300. |
| Over $3,400 but not over $4,400 ................ | $132, plus 14% of the excess over $3,400. |
| Over $4,400 but not over $6,500 ................ | $272, plus 16% of the excess over $4,400. |
| Over $6,500 but not over $8,500 ................ | $608, plus 17% of the excess over $6,500. |
| Over $8,500 but not over $10,800 .............. | $948, plus 19% of the excess over $8,500. |
| Over $10,800 but not over $12,900 ............ | $1,385, plus 22% of the excess over $10,800. |
| Over $12,900 but not over $15,000 ............ | $1,847, plus 23% of the excess over $12,900. |
| Over $15,000 but not over $18,200 ............ | $2,330, plus 27% of the excess over $15,000. |
| Over $18,200 but not over $23,500 ............ | $3,194, plus 31% of the excess over $18,200. |
| Over $23,500 but not over $28,800 ............ | $4,837, plus 35% of the excess over $23,500. |
| Over $28,800 but not over $34,100 ............ | $6,692, plus 40% of the excess over $28,800. |
| Over $34,100 but not over $41,500 ............ | $8,812, plus 44% of the excess over $34,100. |
| Over $41,500 ................................................. | $12,068, plus 50% of the excess over $41,500. |

## "(2) FOR TAXABLE YEARS BEGINNING IN 1983.—

| "If taxable income is: | The tax is: |
|---|---|
| Not over $2,300 | No tax. |
| Over $2,300 but not over $3,400 | 11% of the excess over $2,300. |
| Over $3,400 but not over $4,400 | $121, plus 13% of the excess over $3,400. |
| Over $4,400 but not over $8,500 | $251, plus 15% of the excess over $4,400. |
| Over $8,500 but not over $10,800 | $866, plus 17% of the excess over $8,500. |
| Over $10,800 but not over $12,900 | $1,257, plus 19% of the excess over $10,800. |
| Over $12,900 but not over $15,000 | $1,656, plus 21% of the excess over $12,900. |
| Over $15,000 but not over $18,200 | $2,097, plus 24% of the excess over $15,000. |
| Over $18,200 but not over $23,500 | $2,865, plus 28% of the excess over $18,200. |
| Over $23,500 but not over $28,800 | $4,349, plus 32% of the excess over $23,500. |
| Over $28,800 but not over $34,100 | $6,045, plus 36% of the excess over $28,800. |
| Over $34,100 but not over $41,500 | $7,953, plus 40% of the excess over $34,100. |
| Over $41,500 but not over $55,300 | $10,913, plus 45% of the excess over $41,500. |
| Over $55,300 | $17,123, plus 50% of the excess over $55,300. |

## "(3) FOR TAXABLE YEARS BEGINNING AFTER 1983.—

| "If taxable income is: | The tax is: |
|---|---|
| Not over $2,300 | No tax. |
| Over $2,300 but not over $3,400 | 11% of the excess over $2,300. |
| Over $3,400 but not over $4,400 | $121, plus 12% of the excess over $3,400. |
| Over $4,400 but not over $6,500 | $241, plus 14% of the excess over $4,400. |
| Over $6,500 but not over $8,500 | $535, plus 15% of the excess over $6,500. |
| Over $8,500 but not over $10,800 | $835, plus 16% of the excess over $8,500. |
| Over $10,800 but not over $12,900 | $1,203, plus 18% of the excess over $10,800. |
| Over $12,900 but not over $15,000 | $1,581, plus 20% of the excess over $12,900. |
| Over $15,000 but not over $18,200 | $2,001, plus 23% of the excess over $15,000. |
| Over $18,200 but not over $23,500 | $2,737, plus 26% of the excess over $18,200. |
| Over $23,500 but not over $28,800 | $4,115, plus 30% of the excess over $23,500. |
| Over $28,800 but not over $34,100 | $5,705, plus 34% of the excess over $28,800. |
| Over $34,100 but not over $41,500 | $7,507, plus 38% of the excess over $34,100. |
| Over $41,500 but not over $55,300 | $10,319, plus 42% of the excess over $41,500. |
| Over $55,300 but not over $81,800 | $16,115, plus 48% of the excess over $55,300. |
| Over $81,800 | $28,835, plus 50% of the excess over $81,800. |

"(d) MARRIED INDIVIDUALS FILING SEPARATE RETURNS.—There is hereby imposed on the taxable income of every married individual (as defined in section 143) who does not make a single return jointly with his spouse under section 6013 a tax determined in accordance with the following tables:

"(1) FOR TAXABLE YEARS BEGINNING IN 1982.—

| "If taxable income is: | The tax is: |
|---|---|
| Not over $1,700 | No tax. |
| Over $1,700 but not over $2,750 | 12% of the excess over $1,700. |
| Over $2,750 but not over $3,800 | $126, plus 14% of the excess over $2,750. |
| Over $3,800 but not over $5,950 | $273, plus 16% of the excess over $3,800. |
| Over $5,950 but not over $8,000 | $617, plus 19% of the excess over $5,950. |
| Over $8,000 but not over $10,100 | $1,006, plus 22% of the excess over $8,000. |
| Over $10,100 but not over $12,300 | $1,468, plus 25% of the excess over $10,100. |
| Over $12,300 but not over $14,950 | $2,018, plus 29% of the excess over $12,300. |
| Over $14,950 but not over $17,600 | $2,787, plus 33% of the excess over $14,950. |
| Over $17,600 but not over $22,900 | $3,661, plus 39% of the excess over $17,600. |
| Over $22,900 but not over $30,000 | $5,728, plus 44% of the excess over $22,900. |
| Over $30,000 but not over $42,800 | $8,852, plus 49% of the excess over $30,000. |
| Over $42,800 | $15,124, plus 50% of the excess over $42,800. |

"(2) FOR TAXABLE YEARS BEGINNING IN 1983.—

| "If taxable income is: | The tax is: |
|---|---|
| Not over $1,700 | No tax. |
| Over $1,700 but not over $2,750 | 11% of the excess over $1,700. |
| Over $2,750 but not over $3,800 | $115, plus 13% of the excess over $2,750. |
| Over $3,800 but not over $5,950 | $252, plus 15% of the excess over $3,800. |
| Over $5,950 but not over $8,000 | $574, plus 17% of the excess over $5,950. |
| Over $8,000 but not over $10,100 | $923, plus 19% of the excess over $8,000. |
| Over $10,100 but not over $12,300 | $1,322, plus 23% of the excess over $10,100. |
| Over $12,300 but not over $14,950 | $1,828, plus 26% of the excess over $12,300. |
| Over $14,950 but not over $17,600 | $2,517, plus 30% of the excess over $14,950. |
| Over $17,600 but not over $22,900 | $3,312, plus 35% of the excess over $17,600. |
| Over $22,900 but not over $30,000 | $5,167, plus 40% of the excess over $22,900. |
| Over $30,000 but not over $42,800 | $8,007, plus 44% of the excess over $30,000. |
| Over $42,800 but not over $54,700 | $13,639, plus 48% of the excess over $42,800. |
| Over $54,700 | $19,351, plus 50% of the excess over $54,700. |

## "(3) FOR TAXABLE YEARS BEGINNING AFTER 1983.—

| "If taxable income is: | The tax is: |
|---|---|
| Not over $1,700 | No tax. |
| Over $1,700 but not over $2,750 | 11% of the excess over $1,700. |
| Over $2,750 but not over $3,800 | $115, plus 12% of the excess over $2,750. |
| Over $3,800 but not over $5,950 | $241, plus 14% of the excess over $3,800. |
| Over $5,950 but not over $8,000 | $542, plus 16% of the excess over $5,950. |
| Over $8,000 but not over $10,100 | $870, plus 18% of the excess over $8,000. |
| Over $10,100 but not over $12,300 | $1,248, plus 22% of the excess over $10,100. |
| Over $12,300 but not over $14,950 | $1,732, plus 25% of the excess over $12,300. |
| Over $14,950 but not over $17,600 | $2,395, plus 28% of the excess over $14,950. |
| Over $17,600 but not over $22,900 | $3,137, plus 33% of the excess over $17,600. |
| Over $22,900 but not over $30,000 | $4,886, plus 38% of the excess over $22,900. |
| Over $30,000 but not over $42,800 | $7,584, plus 42% of the excess over $30,000. |
| Over $42,800 but not over $54,700 | $12,960, plus 45% of the excess over $42,800. |
| Over $54,700 but not over $81,200 | $18,315, plus 49% of the excess over $54,700. |
| Over $81,200 | $31,300, plus 50% of the excess over $81,200. |

"(e) ESTATES AND TRUSTS.—There is hereby imposed on the taxable income of every estate and trust taxable under this subsection a tax determined in accordance with the following tables:

## "(1) FOR TAXABLE YEARS BEGINNING IN 1982.—

| "If taxable income is: | The tax is: |
|---|---|
| Not over $1,050 | 12% of taxable income. |
| Over $1,050 but not over $2,100 | $126, plus 14% of the excess over $1,050. |
| Over $2,100 but not over $4,250 | $273, plus 16% of the excess over $2,100. |
| Over $4,250 but not over $6,300 | $617, plus 19% of the excess over $4,250. |
| Over $6,300 but not over $8,400 | $1,006, plus 22% of the excess over $6,300. |
| Over $8,400 but not over $10,600 | $1,468, plus 25% of the excess over $8,400. |
| Over $10,600 but not over $13,250 | $2,018, plus 29% of the excess over $10,600. |
| Over $13,250 but not over $15,900 | $2,787, plus 33% of the excess over $13,250. |
| Over $15,900 but not over $21,200 | $3,661, plus 39% of the excess over $15,900. |
| Over $21,200 but not over $28,300 | $5,728, plus 44% of the excess over $21,200. |
| Over $28,300 but not over $41,100 | $8,852, plus 49% of the excess over $28,300. |
| Over $41,100 | $15,124, plus 50% of the excess over $41,100. |

## "(2) For taxable years beginning in 1983.—

| "If taxable income is: | The tax is: |
|---|---|
| Not over $1,050 | 11% of taxable income. |
| Over $1,050 but not over $2,100 | $115, plus 13% of the excess over $1,050. |
| Over $2,100 but not over $4,250 | $252, plus 15% of the excess over $2,100. |
| Over $4,250 but not over $6,300 | $574, plus 17% of the excess over $4,250. |
| Over $6,300 but not over $8,400 | $923, plus 19% of the excess over $6,300. |
| Over $8,400 but not over $10,600 | $1,322, plus 23% of the excess over $8,400. |
| Over $10,600 but not over $13,250 | $1,828, plus 26% of the excess over $10,600. |
| Over $13,250 but not over $15,900 | $2,517, plus 30% of the excess over $13,250. |
| Over $15,900 but not over $21,200 | $3,312, plus 35% of the excess over $15,900. |
| Over $21,200 but not over $28,300 | $5,167, plus 40% of the excess over $21,200. |
| Over $28,300 but not over $41,100 | $8,007, plus 44% of the excess over $28,300. |
| Over $41,100 but not over $53,000 | $13,639, plus 48% of the excess over $41,100. |
| Over $53,000 | $19,351, plus 50% of the excess over $53,000. |

## "(3) For taxable years beginning after 1983.—

| "If taxable income is: | The tax is: |
|---|---|
| Not over $1,050 | 11% of taxable income. |
| Over $1,050 but not over $2,100 | $115, plus 12% of the excess over $1,050. |
| Over $2,100 but not over $4,250 | $241, plus 14% of the excess over $2,100. |
| Over $4,250 but not over $6,300 | $542, plus 16% of the excess over $4,250. |
| Over $6,300 but not over $8,400 | $870, plus 18% of the excess over $6,300. |
| Over $8,400 but not over $10,600 | $1,248, plus 22% of the excess over $8,400. |
| Over $10,600 but not over $13,250 | $1,732, plus 25% of the excess over $10,600. |
| Over $13,250 but not over $15,900 | $2,395, plus 28% of the excess over $13,250. |
| Over $15,900 but not over $21,200 | $3,137, plus 33% of the excess over $15,900. |
| Over $21,200 but not over $28,300 | $4,886, plus 38% of the excess over $21,200. |
| Over $28,300 but not over $41,100 | $7,584, plus 42% of the excess over $28,300. |
| Over $41,100 but not over $53,000 | $12,960, plus 45% of the excess over $41,100. |
| Over $53,000 but not over $79,500 | $18,315, plus 49% of the excess over $53,000. |
| Over $79,500 | $31,300, plus 50% of the excess over $79,500." |

(b) Credit To Reflect Equivalent 1981 Rate Reduction.—
    (1) In general.—Section 6428 (relating to refund of 1974 individual income taxes) is amended to read as follows:

"SEC. 6428. 1981 RATE REDUCTION TAX CREDIT.

"(a) ALLOWANCE OF CREDIT.—There shall be allowed as a credit against the tax imposed by section 1, or against a tax imposed in lieu of the tax imposed by section 1, for any taxable year beginning in 1981, an amount equal to the product of—

"(1) 1.25 percent, multiplied by

"(2) the amount of tax imposed by section 1 (or in lieu thereof) for such taxable year.

"(b) SPECIAL RULES FOR APPLICATION OF THIS SECTION.—

"(1) APPLICATION WITH OTHER CREDITS.—In determining any credit allowed under subpart A of part IV of subchapter A of chapter 1 (other than under sections 31, 39, and 43), the tax imposed by chapter 1 shall (before any other reductions) be reduced by the credit allowed under subsection (a).

"(2) CREDIT TREATED AS SUBPART A CREDIT.—For purposes of this title, the credit allowed under subsection (a) shall be treated as a credit allowed under subpart A of part IV of subchapter A of chapter 1.

"(c) TABLES TO REFLECT CREDIT.—

"(1) SECTION 3 TABLES.—The tables prescribed by the Secretary under section 3 shall reflect the credit allowed under subsection (a).

"(2) OTHER TABLES.—In order to reflect the amount of the credit under subsection (a) for different levels of tax or taxable income, the Secretary may—

"(A) modify the tables under section 1, or

"(B) prescribe such other tables as he determines necessary."

(2) CONFORMING AMENDMENTS.—

(A) The table of sections for subchapter B of chapter 65 is amended by striking out the item relating to section 6428 and inserting in lieu thereof the following new item:

"Sec. 6428. 1981 rate reduction tax credit."

(B) Paragraph (1) of section 3(a) (relating to imposition of tax table tax) is amended by inserting "and which shall be in such form as he determines appropriate" after "Secretary".

(C) Subsection (a) of section 3 (relating to tax tables for individuals) is amended by adding at the end thereof the following new paragraph:

"(5) SECTION MAY BE APPLIED ON THE BASIS OF TAXABLE INCOME.—The Secretary may provide that this section shall be applied for any taxable year on the basis of taxable income in lieu of tax table income."

(c) REPEAL OF MAXIMUM TAX ON PERSONAL SERVICE INCOME.—

(1) IN GENERAL.—Part VI of subchapter Q of chapter 1 (relating to maximum rate on personal service income) is repealed.

(2) CONFORMING AMENDMENTS.—

(A) Paragraph (1) of section 3(b) (relating to tax tables for individuals) is amended to read as follows:

"(1) an individual to whom section 1301 (relating to income averaging) applies for the taxable year,".

(B) Subsection (b) of section 1304 (relating to special rules for income averaging) is amended—

(i) by inserting "and" at the end of paragraph (1),

(ii) by striking out ", and" at the end of paragraph (2) and inserting in lieu thereof a period, and

(iii) by striking out paragraph (3).

(C) The table of parts for subchapter Q of chapter 1 is amended by striking out the item relating to part VI.

(d) CONFORMING AMENDMENTS.—

(1) ALTERNATIVE MINIMUM TAX.—Paragraph (1) of section 55(a) (relating to alternative minimum tax) is amended—

(A) by striking out all that follows "$60,000" in subparagraph (B) and inserting in lieu thereof ", exceeds", and

(B) by striking out subparagraph (C).

(2) PERSONAL HOLDING COMPANY TAX.—Section 541 (relating to personal holding company tax) is amended by striking out "70 percent" and inserting in lieu thereof "50 percent".

(3) AMENDMENT TO SECTION 21.—Section 21 (relating to effect of changes in rates during taxable year) is amended by striking out subsections (d), (e), and (f) and inserting in lieu thereof the following:

"(d) SECTION NOT TO APPLY TO SECTION 1 RATE CHANGES MADE BY ECONOMIC RECOVERY TAX ACT OF 1981.—This section shall not apply to any change in rates under section 1 attributable to the amendments made by section 101 of the Economic Recovery Tax Act of 1981 or subsection (f) of section 1 (relating to adjustments in tax tables so that inflation will not result in tax increases)."

(e) WITHHOLDING TABLES.—

(1) DETERMINATION OF WITHHOLDING.—Section 3402(a) (relating to requirement of withholding income tax at source) is amended to read as follows:

"(a) REQUIREMENT OF WITHHOLDING.—

"(1) IN GENERAL.—Except as otherwise provided in this section, every employer making payment of wages shall deduct and withhold upon such wages a tax determined in accordance with tables or computational procedures prescribed by the Secretary. Any tables or procedures prescribed under this paragraph shall—

"(A) apply with respect to the amount of wages paid during such periods as the Secretary may prescribe, and

"(B) be in such form, and provide for such amounts to be deducted and withheld, as the Secretary determines to be most appropriate to carry out the purposes of this chapter and to reflect the provisions of chapter 1 applicable to such periods.

"(2) AMOUNT OF WAGES.—For purposes of applying tables or

procedures prescribed under paragraph (1), the term 'the amount of wages' means the amount by which the wages exceed the number of withholding exemptions claimed multiplied by the amount of one such exemption. The amount of each withholding exemption shall be equal to the amount of one personal exemption provided in section 151(b), prorated to the payroll period. The maximum number of withholding exemptions permitted shall be calculated in accordance with regulations prescribed by the Secretary under this section, taking into account any reduction in withholding to which an employee is entitled under this section.

"(3) CHANGES MADE BY SECTION 101 OF THE ECONOMIC RECOVERY TAX ACT OF 1981.—Notwithstanding the provisions of this subsection, the Secretary shall modify the tables and procedures under paragraph (1) to reflect—

"(A) the amendments made by section 101(b) of the Economic Recovery Tax Act of 1981, and such modification shall take effect on October 1, 1981, as if such amendments made a 5-percent reduction effective on such date, and

"(B) the amendments made by section 101(a) of such Act, and such modifications shall take effect—

"(i) on July 1, 1982, as if the reductions in the rate of tax under section 1 (as amended by such section) were attributable to a 10-percent reduction effective on such date, and

"(ii) on July 1, 1983, as if such reductions were attributable to a 10-percent reduction effective on such date."

(2) WAGES PAID FOR PERIOD LESS THAN 1 WEEK.—Section 3402(b) (relating to the percentage method of withholding) is amended—

(A) by striking out paragraph (1), and redesignating paragraphs (2) through (5) as paragraphs (1) through (4), respectively; and

(B) by striking out paragraph (3), as redesignated by subparagraph (A), and inserting in lieu thereof the following:

"(3) In any case in which the period, or the time described in paragraph (2), in respect of any wages is less than one week, the Secretary, under regulations prescribed by him, may authorize an employer to compute the tax to be deducted and withheld as if the aggregate of the wages paid to the employee during the calendar week were paid for a weekly payroll period."

(3) ZERO BRACKET AMOUNT.—Paragraph (1)(G) of section 3402(f) (relating to withholding exemptions) is amended by inserting "(or more than one exemption if so prescribed by the Secretary)" after "one exemption".

(4) CHANGES IN WITHHOLDING.—Section 3402(i) (relating to additional withholding) is amended to read as follows:

"(i) CHANGES IN WITHHOLDING.—

"(1) IN GENERAL.—The Secretary may by regulations provide for increases or decreases in the amount of withholding otherwise required under this section in cases where the employee requests such changes.

"(2) TREATMENT AS TAX.—Any increased withholding under paragraph (1) shall for all purposes be considered tax required to be deducted and withheld under this chapter."

(5) WITHHOLDING ALLOWANCES.—Subsection (m) of section 3402 (relating to withholding allowances based on itemized deductions) is amended to read as follows:

"(m) WITHHOLDING ALLOWANCES.—Under regulations prescribed by the Secretary, an employee shall be entitled to additional withholding allowances or additional reductions in withholding under this subsection. In determining the number of additional withholding allowances or the amount of additional reductions in withholding under this subsection, the employee may take into account (to the extent and in the manner provided by such regulations)—

"(1) estimated itemized deductions allowable under chapter 1 (other than the deductions referred to in section 151 and other than the deductions required to be taken into account in determining adjusted gross income under section 62) (other than paragraph (13) thereof),

"(2) estimated tax credits allowable under chapter 1, and

"(3) such additional deductions and other items as may be specified by the Secretary in regulations."

(f) EFFECTIVE DATES.—

(1) IN GENERAL.—The amendments made by subsections (a), (c), and (d) shall apply to taxable years beginning after December 31, 1981.

(2) WITHHOLDING AMENDMENTS.—The amendments made by subsection (e) shall apply to remuneration paid after September 30, 1981; except that the amendment made by subsection (e)(5) shall apply to remuneration paid after December 31, 1981.


# Reduction of Capital Gain Tax Rate for Individuals

(Section 102)


(a) IN GENERAL.—If for any taxable year ending after June 9, 1981, and beginning before January 1, 1982, a taxpayer other than a corporation has qualified net capital gain, then the tax imposed under section 1 of the Internal Revenue Code of 1954 for such taxable year shall be equal to the lesser of—

(1) the tax imposed under such section determined without regard to this subsection, or

(2) the sum of—
    (A) the tax imposed under such section on the excess of—
        (i) the taxable income of the taxpayer, over
        (ii) 40 percent of the qualified net capital gain of the taxpayer, and
    (B) 20 percent of the qualified net capital gain.

(b) APPLICATION WITH ALTERNATIVE MINIMUM TAX.—
    (1) IN GENERAL.—If subsection (a) applies to any taxpayer for any taxable year, then the amount determined under section 55(a)(1) of the Internal Revenue Code of 1954 for such taxable year shall be equal to the lesser of—
        (A) the amount determined under such section 55(a)(1) determined without regard to this subsection, or
        (B) the sum of—
            (i) the amount which would be determined under such section 55(a)(1) if the alternative minimum taxable income was the excess of—
                (I) the alternative minimum taxable income (within the meaning of section 55(b)(1) of such Code) of the taxpayer, over
                (II) the qualified net capital gain of the taxpayer, and
            (ii) 20 percent of the qualified net capital gain.
    (2) NO CREDITS ALLOWABLE.—For purposes of section 55(c) of such Code, no credit allowable under subpart A of part IV of subchapter A of chapter 1 of such Code (other than section 33(a) of such Code) shall be allowable against the amount described in paragraph (1)(B)(ii).

(c) QUALIFIED NET CAPITAL GAIN.—
    (1) IN GENERAL.—For purposes of this section, the term "qualified net capital gain" means the lesser of—
        (A) the net capital gain for the taxable year, or
        (B) the net capital gain for the taxable year taking into account only gain or loss from sales or exchanges occurring after June 9, 1981.
    (2) NET CAPITAL GAIN.—For purposes of this subsection, the term "net capital gain" has the meaning given such term by section 1222(11) of the Internal Revenue Code of 1954.

(d) SPECIAL RULE FOR PASS-THRU ENTITIES.—
    (1) IN GENERAL.—In applying subsections (a), (b), and (c) with respect to any pass-thru entity, the determination of when a sale or exchange has occurred shall be made at the entity level.
    (2) PASS-THRU ENTITY DEFINED.—For purposes of paragraph (1), the term "pass-thru entity" means—
        (A) a regulated investment company,
        (B) a real estate investment trust,
        (C) an electing small business corporation,
        (D) a partnership,
        (E) an estate or trust, and
        (F) a common trust fund.

# Indexing

(Section 104)

(a) ADJUSTMENTS TO INDIVIDUAL INCOME TAX BRACKETS.—Section 1 (relating to tax imposed) is amended by adding at the end thereof the following new subsection:

"(f) ADJUSTMENTS IN TAX TABLES SO THAT INFLATION WILL NOT RESULT IN TAX INCREASES.—

"(1) IN GENERAL.—Not later than December 15 of 1984 and each subsequent calendar year, the Secretary shall prescribe tables which shall apply in lieu of the tables contained in paragraph (3) of subsections (a), (b), (c), (d), and (e) with respect to taxable years beginning in the succeeding calendar year.

"(2) METHOD OF PRESCRIBING TABLES.—The table which under paragraph (1) is to apply in lieu of the table contained in paragraph (3) of subsection (a), (b), (c), (d), or (e), as the case may be, with respect to taxable years beginning in any calendar year shall be prescribed—

"(A) by increasing—
"(i) the maximum dollar amount on which no tax is imposed under such table, and
"(ii) the minimum and maximum dollar amounts for each rate bracket for which a tax is imposed under such table,
by the cost-of-living adjustment for such calendar year,
"(B) by not changing the rate applicable to any rate bracket as adjusted under subparagraph (A)(ii), and
"(C) by adjusting the amounts setting forth the tax to the extent necessary to reflect the adjustments in the rate brackets.

If any increase determined under subparagraph (A) is not a multiple of $10, such increase shall be rounded to the nearest multiple of $10 (or if such increase is a multiple of $5, such increase shall be increased to the next highest multiple of $10).

"(3) COST-OF-LIVING ADJUSTMENT.—For purposes of paragraph (2), the cost-of-living adjustment for any calendar year is the percentage (if any) by which—
"(A) the CPI for the preceding calendar year, exceeds
"(B) the CPI for the calendar year 1983.

"(4) CPI FOR ANY CALENDAR YEAR.—For purposes of paragraph (3), the CPI for any calendar year is the average of the Consumer Price Index as of the close of the 12-month period ending on September 30 of such calendar year.

"(5) CONSUMER PRICE INDEX.—For purposes of paragraph (4), the term 'Consumer Price Index' means the last Consumer Price Index for all-urban consumers published by the Department of Labor."

(b) DEFINITION OF ZERO BRACKET AMOUNT.—Subsection (d) of section 63 (defining zero bracket amount) is amended to read as follows:

"(d) ZERO BRACKET AMOUNT.—For purposes of this subtitle, the term 'zero bracket amount' means—

"(1) in the case of an individual to whom subsection (a), (b), (c), or (d) of section 1 applies, the maximum amount of taxable income on which no tax is imposed by the applicable subsection of section 1, or

"(2) zero in any other case."

(c) PERSONAL EXEMPTIONS.—

(1) GENERAL RULE.—Section 151 (relating to allowance of deductions for personal exemptions) is amended by striking out "$1,000" each place it appears and inserting in lieu thereof "the exemption amount".

(2) EXEMPTION AMOUNT.—Section 151 is amended by adding at the end thereof the following new subsection:

"(f) EXEMPTION AMOUNT.—For purposes of this section, the term 'exemption amount' means, with respect to any taxable year, $1,000 increased by an amount equal to $1,000 multiplied by the cost-of-living adjustment (as defined in section 1(f)(3)) for the calendar year in which the taxable year begins. If the amount determined under the preceding sentence is not a multiple of $10, such amount shall be rounded to the nearest multiple of $10 (or if such amount is a multiple of $5, such amount shall be increased to the next highest multiple of $10)."

(d) RETURN REQUIREMENTS.—

(1) AMENDMENTS TO SECTION 6012.—

(A) Clause (i) of section 6012(a)(1)(A) is amended by striking out "$3,300" and inserting in lieu thereof "the sum of the exemption amount plus the zero bracket amount applicable to such an individual".

(B) Clause (ii) of section 6012(a)(1)(A) is amended by striking out "$4,400" and inserting in lieu thereof "the sum of the exemption amount plus the zero bracket amount applicable to such an individual".

(C) Clause (iii) of section 6012(a)(1)(A) is amended by striking out "$5,400" and inserting in lieu thereof "the sum of twice the exemption amount plus the zero bracket amount applicable to a joint return".

(D) Paragraph (1) of section 6012(a) is amended by striking out "$1,000" each place it appears and inserting in lieu thereof "the exemption amount".

(E) Paragraph (1) of section 6012(a) is amended by adding at the end thereof the following new subparagraph:

"(D) For purposes of this paragraph—

"(i) The term 'zero bracket amount' has the meaning given to such term by section 63(d).

"(ii) The term 'exemption amount' has the meaning

given to such term by section 151(f)."

(2) AMENDMENTS TO SECTION 6013.—Subparagraph (A) of section 6013(b)(3) is amended—

(A) by striking out "$1,000" each place it appears and inserting in lieu thereof "the exemption amount",

(B) by striking out "$2,000" each place it appears and inserting in lieu thereof "twice the exemption amount", and

(C) by adding at the end thereof the following new sentence: "For purposes of this subparagraph, the term 'exemption amount' has the meaning given to such term by section 151(f)."

(e) EFFECTIVE DATE.—The amendments made by this section shall apply to taxable years beginning after December 31, 1984.

## Charitable Deduction for Non-Itemizers

(Section 121)

(a) IN GENERAL.—Section 170 (relating to charitable, etc., contributions and gifts) is amended by redesignating subsections (i) and (j) as subsections (j) and (k), respectively, and by inserting after subsection (h) the following new subsection:

"(i) RULE FOR NONITEMIZATION OF DEDUCTIONS.—

"(1) IN GENERAL.—In the case of an individual who does not itemize his deductions for the taxable year, the applicable percentage of the amount allowable under subsection (a) for the taxable year shall be taken into account as a direct charitable deduction under section 63.

"(2) APPLICABLE PERCENTAGE.—For purposes of paragraph (1), the applicable percentage shall be determined under the following table:

| "For taxable years beginning in— | The applicable percentage is— |
|---|---|
| 1982, 1983 or 1984 | 25 |
| 1985 | 50 |
| 1986 or thereafter | 100. |

"(3) LIMITATION FOR TAXABLE YEARS BEGINNING BEFORE 1985.—In the case of a taxable year beginning before 1985, the portion of the amount allowable under subsection (a) to which the applicable percentage shall be applied—

"(A) shall not exceed $100 for taxable years beginning in 1982 or 1983, and

"(B) shall not exceed $300 for taxable years beginning in 1984.

In the case of a married individual filing a separate return, the limit under subparagraph (A) shall be $50, and the limit under subparagraph (B) shall be $150.

"(4) TERMINATION.—The provisions of this subsection shall not apply to contributions made after December 31, 1986."

(b) DEFINITION OF TAXABLE INCOME.—

(1) IN GENERAL.—Paragraph (1) of section 63(b) (relating to individuals) is amended—

(A) by striking out "and" at the end of subparagraph (A), and

(B) by inserting after subparagraph (B) the following new subparagraph:

"(C) the direct charitable deduction, and".

(2) DIRECT CHARITABLE DEDUCTION DEFINED.—Section 63 (defining taxable income) is amended by adding at the end thereof the following new subsection:

"(i) DIRECT CHARITABLE DEDUCTION.—For purposes of this section, the term 'direct charitable deduction' means that portion of the amount allowable under section 170(a) which is taken as a direct charitable deduction for the taxable year under section 170(i)."

(c) CONFORMING AMENDMENTS.—

(1) Paragraph (1) of section 57(b) (relating to adjusted itemized deductions) is amended by inserting "without regard to paragraph (3) thereof" after "section 63(f)".

(2) Subsection (f) of section 63 (relating to itemized deductions) is amended—

(A) by striking out "and" at the end of paragraph (1),

(B) by striking out the period at the end of paragraph (2) and inserting in lieu thereof ", and", and

(C) by adding at the end thereof the following new paragraph:

"(3) the direct charitable deduction."

(3) Subparagraph (A) of section 3(a)(4) (relating to imposition of tax table tax) is amended to read as follows:

"(A) reduced by the sum of—

"(i) the excess itemized deductions, and

"(ii) the direct charitable deduction, and".

(d) EFFECTIVE DATE.—The amendments made by this section shall apply to contributions made after December 31, 1981, in taxable years beginning after such date.


## Two-Year Period for Rollover of Personal Residence

(Section 122)

(a) IN GENERAL.—Section 1034 (relating to rollover of gain on sale of principal residence) is amended by striking out "18 months" each place it appears and inserting in lieu thereof "2 years".

(b) CONFORMING AMENDMENTS.—

(1) Paragraph (4) of section 1034(c) is amended by striking out

"18-month" and inserting in lieu thereof "2-year".

(2) Paragraph (5) of section 1034(c) is hereby repealed.

(c) EFFECTIVE DATE.—The amendments made by this section shall apply to old residences (within the meaning of section 1034 of the Internal Revenue Code of 1954) sold or exchanged—

(1) after July 20, 1981, or

(2) on or before such date, if the rollover period under such section (determined without regard to the amendments made by this section) expires on or after such date.

## One-Time Exclusion of Gain on Sale of Personal Residence

(Section 123)

(a) IN GENERAL.—Paragraph (1) of section 121(b) (relating to one-time exclusion of gain from sale of principal residence by individual who has attained age 55) is amended by striking out "$100,000 ($50,000" and inserting in lieu thereof "$125,000 ($62,500".

(b) EFFECTIVE DATE.—The amendment made by this section shall apply to residences sold or exchanged after July 20, 1981.

## Tax Rates for Principal Campaign Committees

(Section 128)

(a) IN GENERAL.—Section 527 (relating to political organizations) is amended by adding at the end thereof the following new subsection:

"(h) SPECIAL RULE FOR PRINCIPAL CAMPAIGN COMMITTEES.—

"(1) IN GENERAL.—In the case of a political organization which is a principal campaign committee, paragraph (1) of subsection (b) shall be applied by substituting 'the appropriate rates' for 'the highest rate'.

"(2) PRINCIPAL CAMPAIGN COMMITTEE DEFINED.—

"(A) IN GENERAL.—For purposes of this subsection, the term 'principal campaign committee' means the political committee designated by a candidate for Congress as his principal campaign committee for purposes of—

"(i) section 302(e) of the Federal Election Campaign Act of 1971 (2 U.S.C. 432(e)), and

"(ii) this subsection.

"(B) DESIGNATION.—A candidate may have only 1 designation in effect under subparagraph (A)(ii) at any time and such designation—

"(i) shall be made at such time and in such manner as the Secretary may prescribe by regulations, and
"(ii) once made, may be revoked only with the consent of the Secretary."
(b) EFFECTIVE DATE.—The amendments made by this section shall apply to taxable years beginning after December 31, 1981.

## Increase in Investment Tax Credit for Qualified Rehabilitation Expenditures

(Section 212)

(a) INCREASE IN AMOUNT OF CREDIT.—
(1) IN GENERAL.—Subparagraph (A) of section 46(a)(2) (relating to amount of investment tax credit) is amended by striking out "and" at the end of clause (ii), by striking out the period at the end of clause (iii), by inserting in lieu thereof ", and", and by adding at the end thereof the following new clause:
"(iv) in the case of that portion of the basis of any property which is attributable to qualified rehabilitation expenditures, the rehabilitation percentage."
(2) REHABILITATION PERCENTAGE DEFINED.—Paragraph (2) of section 46(a) is amended by adding at the end thereof the following new subparagraph:
"(F) REHABILITATION PERCENTAGE.—For purposes of this paragraph—
"(i) IN GENERAL.—

| "In the case of qualified rehabilitation expenditures with respect to a: | The rehabilitation percentage is: |
|---|---|
| 30-year building | 15 |
| 40-year building | 20 |
| Certified historic structure | 25. |

"(ii) REGULAR AND ENERGY PERCENTAGES NOT TO APPLY.—The regular percentage and the energy percentage shall not apply to that portion of the basis of any property which is attributable to qualified rehabilitation expenditures.
"(iii) DEFINITIONS.—
"(I) 30-YEAR BUILDING.—The term '30-year building' means a qualified rehabilitated building other than a 40-year building and other than a certified historic structure.
"(II) 40-YEAR BUILDING.—The term '40-year building' means any building (other than a certified

historic structure) which would meet the requirements of section 48(g)(1)(B) if '40' were substituted for '30' each place it appears in subparagraph (B) thereof.

"(III) CERTIFIED HISTORIC STRUCTURE.—The term 'certified historic structure' has the meaning given to such term by section 48(g)(3)."

(3) CONFORMING AMENDMENT.—Section 48(o) (defining certain credits) is amended by adding at the end thereof the following new paragraph:

"(8) REHABILITATION INVESTMENT CREDIT.—The term 'rehabilitation investment credit' means that portion of the credit allowable by section 38 which is attributable to the rehabilitation percentage."

(b) QUALIFIED REHABILITATED BUILDINGS AND EXPENDITURES.—Subsection (g) of section 48 (relating to special rules for qualified rehabilitated buildings) is amended to read as follows:

"(g) SPECIAL RULES FOR QUALIFIED REHABILITATED BUILDINGS.—For purposes of this subpart—

"(1) QUALIFIED REHABILITATED BUILDING DEFINED.—

"(A) IN GENERAL.—The term 'qualified rehabilitated building' means any building (and its structural components)—

"(i) which has been substantially rehabilitated,

"(ii) which was placed in service before the beginning of the rehabilitation, and

"(iii) 75 percent or more of the existing external walls of which are retained in place as external walls in the rehabilitation process.

"(B) 30 YEARS MUST HAVE ELAPSED SINCE CONSTRUCTION.—In the case of a building other than a certified historic structure, a building shall not be a qualified rehabilitated building unless there is a period of at least 30 years between the date the physical work on the rehabilitation began and the date the building was first placed in service.

"(C) SUBSTANTIALLY REHABILITATED DEFINED.—

"(i) IN GENERAL.—For purposes of subparagraph (A)(i), a building shall be treated as having been substantially rehabilitated only if the qualified rehabilitation expenditures during the 24-month period ending on the last day of the taxable year exceed the greater of—

"(I) the adjusted basis of such property, or

"(II) $5,000.

The adjusted basis of the property shall be determined as of the beginning of the first day of such 24-month period, or of the holding period of the property (within the meaning of section 1250(e)), whichever is later.

"(ii) SPECIAL RULE FOR PHASED REHABILITATION.—In the case of any rehabilitation which may reasonably be expected to be completed in phases set forth in architectural plans and specifications completed before the rehabilitation begins, clause (i) shall be applied by substituting '60-month period' for '24-month period'.

"(iii) LESSEES.—The Secretary shall prescribe by regulation rules for applying this provision to lessees.

"(D) RECONSTRUCTION.—Rehabilitation includes reconstruction.

"(2) QUALIFIED REHABILITATION EXPENDITURE DEFINED.—

"(A) IN GENERAL.—The term 'qualified rehabilitation expenditure' means any amount properly chargeable to capital account which is incurred after December 31, 1981—

"(i) for property (or additions or improvements to property) which have a recovery period (within the meaning of section 168) of 15 years, and

"(ii) in connection with the rehabilitation of a qualified rehabilitated building.

"(B) CERTAIN EXPENDITURES NOT INCLUDED.—The term 'qualified rehabilitation expenditure' does not include—

"(i) ACCELERATED METHODS OF DEPRECIATION MAY NOT BE USED.—Any expenditures with respect to which an election has not been made under section 168(b)(3) (to use the straight-line method of depreciation).

"(ii) COST OF ACQUISITION.—The cost of acquiring any building or interest therein.

"(iii) ENLARGEMENTS.—Any expenditure attributable to the enlargement of an existing building.

"(iv) CERTIFIED HISTORIC STRUCTURE, ETC.—Any expenditure attributable to the rehabilitation of a certified historic structure or a building in a registered historic district, unless the rehabilitation is a certified rehabilitation (within the meaning of subparagraph (C)). The preceding sentence shall not apply to a building in a registered historic district if—

"(I) such building was not a certified historic structure,

"(II) the Secretary of the Interior certified to the Secretary that such building is not of historic significance to the district, and

"(III) if the certification referred to in subclause (II) occurs after the beginning of the rehabilitation of such building, the taxpayer certifies to the Secretary that, at the beginning of such rehabilitation, he in good faith was not aware of the requirements of subclause (II).

"(v) EXPENDITURES OF LESSEE.—Any expenditure of a lessee of a building if, on the date the rehabilitation is completed, the remaining term of the lease (determined without regard to any renewal periods) is less than 15 years.

"(C) CERTIFIED REHABILITATION.—For purposes of subparagraph (B), the term 'certified rehabilitation' means any rehabilitation of a certified historic structure which the Secretary of the Interior has certified to the Secretary as being consistent with the historic character of such property or the district in which such property is located.

"(3) CERTIFIED HISTORIC STRUCTURE DEFINED.—

"(A) IN GENERAL.—The term 'certified historic structure' means any building (and its structural components) which—

"(i) is listed in the National Register, or

"(ii) is located in a registered historic district and is certified by the Secretary of the Interior to the Secretary as being of historic significance to the district.

"(B) REGISTERED HISTORIC DISTRICT.—The term 'registered historic district' means—

"(i) any district listed in the National Register, and

"(ii) any district—

"(I) which is designated under a statute of the appropriate State or local government, if such statute is certified by the Secretary of the Interior to the Secretary as containing criteria which will substantially achieve the purpose of preserving and rehabilitating buildings of historic significance to the district, and

"(II) which is certified by the Secretary of the Interior to the Secretary as meeting substantially all of the requirements for the listing of districts in the National Register.

"(4) PROPERTY TREATED AS NEW SECTION 38 PROPERTY.—Property which is treated as section 38 property by reason of subsection (a)(1)(E) shall be treated as new section 38 property.

"(5) ADJUSTMENT TO BASIS.—

"(A) IN GENERAL.—For purposes of this subtitle, if a credit is allowed under this section for any qualified rehabilitation expenditure in connection with a qualified rehabilitated building other than a certified historic structure, the increase in basis of such property which would (but for this paragraph) result from such expenditure shall be reduced by the amount of the credit so allowed.

"(B) CERTAIN DISPOSITIONS.—If during any taxable year there is a recapture amount determined with respect to any qualified rehabilitated building the basis of which was reduced under subparagraph (A), the basis of such building (immediately before the event resulting in such recapture) shall be increased by an amount equal to such recapture amount. For purposes of the preceding sentence, the term 'recapture amount' means any increase in tax (or adjustment in carrybacks or carryovers) determined under section 47(a)(5)."

(c) LODGING TO QUALIFY.—Paragraph (3) of section 48(a) (relating to property used for lodging) is amended—

(1) by striking out "and" at the end of subparagraph (B),

(2) by striking out the period at the end of subparagraph (C) and inserting in lieu thereof ", and", and

(3) by adding at the end thereof the following new subparagraph:

"(D) a certified historic structure to the extent of that portion of the basis which is attributable to qualified rehabilitation expenditures."

(d) REPEAL OF CERTAIN PROVISIONS RELATING TO HISTORIC STRUCTURES.—

(1) IN GENERAL.—Section 191 (relating to amortization of certain rehabilitation expenditures for certified historic structures) and subsections (n) and (o) of section 167 (relating to depreciation) are hereby repealed.

(2) CONFORMING AMENDMENTS.—

(A) Paragraph (8) of section 48(a) (relating to amortized property) is amended by striking out "188, or 191" and inserting in lieu thereof "or 188".

(B) Paragraph (2) of section 57(a) (relating to items of tax preference) is amended by striking out "or 191".

(C) Section 280B (relating to demolition of certain historic structures) is amended—

(i) by striking out "section 191(d)(1)" in subsection (a), and inserting in lieu thereof "48(g)(3)(A)", and

(ii) by striking out "section 191(d)(2)" in subsection (b) and inserting in lieu thereof "section 48(g)(3)(B)".

(D) Subsection (f) of section 642 (relating to special rules for credits and deductions) is amended by striking out "188, and 191" and inserting in lieu thereof "and 188".

(E) Subparagraph (B) of section 1082(a)(2) (relating to basis for determining gain or loss) is amended by striking out "188, or 191" and inserting in lieu thereof "or 188".

(F) Paragraph (2) of section 1245(a) (relating to gain from dispositions of certain depreciable property) and paragraph (4) of section 1250(b) (relating to gain from dispositions of certain depreciable realty) are each amended by inserting "(as in effect before its repeal by the Economic Recovery Tax Act of 1981)" after "191" each place it appears.

(G) Subsection (a) of section 1016 (relating to adjustments to basis) is amended—

(i) by striking out "and" at the end of paragraph (22),

(ii) by striking out the period at the end of paragraph (23) and inserting in lieu thereof ", and", and

(iii) by adding at the end thereof the following new paragraph:

"(24) to the extent provided in section 48(g)(5), in the case of expenditures with respect to which a credit has been allowed under section 38."

(e) EFFECTIVE DATES.—

(1) IN GENERAL.—Except as provided in paragraph (2), the amendments made by this section shall apply to expenditures incurred after December 31, 1981, in taxable years ending after such date.

(2) TRANSITIONAL RULE.—The amendments made by this section shall not apply with respect to any rehabilitation of a building if—

(A) the physical work on such rehabilitation began before January 1, 1982, and

(B) such building meets the requirements of paragraph (1) of section 48(g) of the Internal Revenue Code of 1954 (as in effect on the day before the date of enactment of this Act) but does not meet the requirements of such paragraph (1) (as amended by this Act).

## Investment Tax Credit for Certain Rehabilitated Buildings Leased to Tax-Exempt Organizations

(Section 214)

(a) USE BY TAX-EXEMPT ORGANIZATIONS.—Paragraph (4) of section 48(a) (relating to property used by certain tax-exempt organizations) is amended by adding at the end thereof the following new sentence: "If any qualified rehabilitated building is used by the tax-exempt organization pursuant to a lease, this paragraph shall not apply to that portion of the basis of such building which is attributable to qualified rehabilitation expenditures."

(b) USE BY GOVERNMENTAL UNITS.—Paragraph (5) of section 48(a) (relating to governmental units) is amended by adding at the end thereof the following new sentence: "If any qualified rehabilitated building is used by the governmental unit pursuant to a lease, this paragraph shall not apply to that portion of the basis of such building which is attributable to qualified rehabilitation expenditures."

(c) EFFECTIVE DATE.—The amendments made by this section shall apply to uses after July 29, 1980, in taxable years ending after such date.

## Tax Credit for Increasing Research Activities

(Section 221)

(a) GENERAL RULE.—Subpart A of part IV of subchapter A of chapter 1 (relating to credits allowable) is amended by inserting after section 44E the following new section:

## "SEC. 44F. CREDIT FOR INCREASING RESEARCH ACTIVITIES.

"(a) GENERAL RULE.—There shall be allowed as a credit against the tax imposed by this chapter for the taxable year an amount equal to 25 percent of the excess (if any) of—

"(1) the qualified research expenses for the taxable year, over

"(2) the base period research expenses.

"(b) QUALIFIED RESEARCH EXPENSES.—For purposes of this section—

"(1) QUALIFIED RESEARCH EXPENSES.—The term 'qualified research expenses' means the sum of the following amounts which are paid or incurred by the taxpayer during the taxable year in carrying on any trade or business of the taxpayer—

"(A) in-house research expenses, and

"(B) contract research expenses.

"(2) IN-HOUSE RESEARCH EXPENSES.—

"(A) IN GENERAL.—The term 'in-house research expenses' means—

"(i) any wages paid or incurred to an employee for qualified services performed by such employee,

"(ii) any amount paid or incurred for supplies used in the conduct of qualified research, and

"(iii) any amount paid or incurred to another person for the right to use personal property in the conduct of qualified research.

"(B) QUALIFIED SERVICES.—The term 'qualified services' means services consisting of—

"(i) engaging in qualified research, or

"(ii) engaging in the direct supervision or direct support of research activities which constitute qualified research.

If substantially all of the services performed by an individual for the taxpayer during the taxable year consists of services meeting the requirements of clause (i) or (ii), the term 'qualified services' means all of the services performed by such individual for the taxpayer during the taxable year.

"(C) SUPPLIES.—The term 'supplies' means any tangible property other than—

"(i) land or improvements to land, and

"(ii) property of a character subject to the allowance for depreciation.

"(D) WAGES.—

"(i) IN GENERAL.—The term 'wages' has the meaning given such term by section 3401(a).

"(ii) SELF-EMPLOYED INDIVIDUALS AND OWNER-EMPLOYEES.—In the case of an employee (within the meaning of section 401(c)(1)), the term 'wages' includes the earned income (as defined in section 401(c)(2)) of such employee.

"(iii) Exclusion for wages to which new jobs or win credit applies.—The term 'wages' shall not include any amount taken into account in computing the credit under section 40 or 44B.

"(3) Contract research expenses.—

"(A) In general.—The term 'contract research expenses' means 65 percent of any amount paid or incurred by the taxpayer to any person (other than an employee of the taxpayer) for qualified research.

"(B) Prepaid amounts.—If any contract research expenses paid or incurred during any taxable year are attributable to qualified research to be conducted after the close of such taxable year, such amount shall be treated as paid or incurred during the period during which the qualified research is conducted.

"(c) Base Period Research Expenses.—For purposes of this section—

"(1) In general.—The term 'base period research expenses' means the average of the qualified research expenses for each year in the base period.

"(2) Base period.—

"(A) In general.—For purposes of this subsection, the term 'base period' means the 3 taxable years immediately preceding the taxable year for which the determination is being made (hereinafter in this subsection referred to as the 'determination year').

"(B) Transitional rules.—Subparagraph (A) shall be applied—

"(i) by substituting 'first taxable year' for '3 taxable years' in the case of the first determination year ending after June 30, 1981, and

"(ii) by substituting '2' for '3' in the case of the second determination year ending after June 30, 1981.

"(3) Minimum base period research expenses.—In no event shall the base period research expenses be less than 50 percent of the qualified research expenses for the determination year.

"(d) Qualified Research.—For purposes of this section the term 'qualified research' has the same meaning as the term research or experimental has under section 174, except that such term shall not include—

"(1) qualified research conducted outside the United States,

"(2) qualified research in the social sciences or humanities, and

"(3) qualified research to the extent funded by any grant, contract, or otherwise by another person (or any governmental entity).

"(e) Credit Available With Respect to Certain Basic Research by Colleges, Universities, and Certain Research Organizations.—

"(1) IN GENERAL.—65 percent of any amount paid or incurred by a corporation (as such term is defined in section 170(e)(4)(D)) to any qualified organization for basic research to be performed by such organization shall be treated as contract research expenses. The preceding sentence shall apply only if the amount is paid or incurred pursuant to a written research agreement between the corporation and the qualified organization.

"(2) QUALIFIED ORGANIZATION.—For purposes of this subsection, the term 'qualified organization' means—

"(A) any educational organization which is described in section 170(b)(1)(A)(ii) and which is an institution of higher education (as defined in section 3304(f)), and

"(B) any other organization which—

"(i) is described in section 501(c)(3) and exempt from tax under section 501(a),

"(ii) is organized and operated primarily to conduct scientific research, and

"(iii) is not a private foundation.

"(3) BASIC RESEARCH.—The term 'basic research' means any original investigation for the advancement of scientific knowledge not having a specific commercial objective, except that such term shall not include—

"(A) basic research conducted outside the United States, and

"(B) basic research in the social sciences or humanities.

"(4) SPECIAL RULES FOR GRANTS TO CERTAIN FUNDS.—

"(A) IN GENERAL.—For purposes of this subsection, a qualified fund shall be treated as a qualified organization and the requirements of paragraph (1) that the basic research be performed by the qualified organization shall not apply.

"(B) QUALIFIED FUND.—For purposes of subparagraph (A), the term 'qualified fund' means any organization which—

"(i) is described in section 501(c)(3) and exempt from tax under section 501(a) and is not a private foundation,

"(ii) is established and maintained by an organization established before July 10, 1981, which meets the requirements of clause (i),

"(iii) is organized and operated exclusively for purposes of making grants pursuant to written research agreements to organizations described in paragraph (2)(A) for purposes of basic research, and

"(iv) makes an election under this paragraph.

"(C) EFFECT OF ELECTION.—

"(i) IN GENERAL.—Any organization which makes an election under this paragraph shall be treated as a private foundation for purposes of this title (other than section 4940, relating to excise tax based on investment income).

"(ii) ELECTION REVOCABLE ONLY WITH CONSENT.—An election under this paragraph, once made, may be revoked only with the consent of the Secretary.

"(f) SPECIAL RULES.—For purposes of this section—

"(1) AGGREGATION OF EXPENDITURES.—

"(A) CONTROLLED GROUP OF CORPORATIONS.—In determining the amount of the credit under this section—

"(i) all members of the same controlled group of corporations shall be treated as a single taxpayer, and

"(ii) the credit (if any) allowable by this section to each such member shall be its proportionate share of the increase in qualified research expenses giving rise to the credit.

"(B) COMMON CONTROL.—Under regulations prescribed by the Secretary, in determining the amount of the credit under this section—

"(i) all trades or businesses (whether or not incorporated) which are under common control shall be treated as a single taxpayer, and

"(ii) the credit (if any) allowable by this section to each such person shall be its proportionate share of the increase in qualified research expenses giving rise to the credit.

The regulations prescribed under this subparagraph shall be based on principles similar to the principles which apply in the case of subparagraph (A).

"(2) ALLOCATIONS.—

"(A) PASSTHROUGH IN THE CASE OF SUBCHAPTER S CORPORATIONS, ETC.—Under regulations prescribed by the Secretary, rules similar to the rules of subsections (d) and (e) of section 52 shall apply.

"(B) ALLOCATION IN THE CASE OF PARTNERSHIPS.—In the case of partnerships, the credit shall be allocated among partners under regulations prescribed by the Secretary.

"(3) ADJUSTMENTS FOR CERTAIN ACQUISITIONS, ETC.—Under regulations prescribed by the Secretary—

"(A) ACQUISITIONS.—If, after June 30, 1980, a taxpayer acquires the major portion of a trade or business of another person (hereinafter in this paragraph referred to as the 'predecessor') or the major portion of a separate unit of a trade or business of a predecessor, then, for purposes of applying this section for any taxable year ending after such acquisition, the amount of qualified research expenses paid or incurred by the taxpayer during periods before such acquisition shall be increased by so much of such expenses paid or incurred by the predecessor with respect to the acquired trade or business as is attributable to the portion of such trade or business or separate unit acquired by the taxpayer.

"(B) DISPOSITIONS.—If, after June 30, 1980—

"(i) a taxpayer disposes of the major portion of any trade or business or the major portion of a separate unit of a trade or business in a transaction to which subparagraph (A) applies, and

"(ii) the taxpayer furnished the acquiring person such information as is necessary for the application of subparagraph (A),

then, for purposes of applying this section for any taxable year ending after such disposition, the amount of qualified research expenses paid or incurred by the taxpayer during periods before such disposition shall be decreased by so much of such expenses as is attributable to the portion of such trade or business or separate unit disposed of by the taxpayer.

"(C) INCREASE IN BASE PERIOD.—If during any of the 3 taxable years following the taxable year in which a disposition to which subparagraph (B) applies occurs, the disposing taxpayer (or a person with whom the taxpayer is required to aggregate expenditures under paragraph (1)) reimburses the acquiring person (or a person required to so aggregate expenditures with such person) for research on behalf of the taxpayer, then the amount of qualified research expenses of the taxpayer for the base period for such taxable year shall be increased by the lesser of—

"(i) the amount of the decrease under subparagraph (B) which is allocable to such base period, or

"(ii) the product of the number of years in the base period, multiplied by the amount of the reimbursement described in this subparagraph.

"(4) SHORT TAXABLE YEARS.—In the case of any short taxable year, qualified research expenses shall be annualized in such circumstances and under such methods as the Secretary may prescribe by regulation.

"(5) CONTROLLED GROUP OF CORPORATIONS.—The term 'controlled group of corporations' has the same meaning given to such term by section 1563(a), except that—

"(A) 'more than 50 percent' shall be substituted for 'at least 80 percent' each place it appears in section 1563(a)(1), and

"(B) the determination shall be made without regard to subsections (a)(4) and (e)(3)(C) of section 1563.

"(g) LIMITATION BASED ON AMOUNT OF TAX.—

"(1) LIABILITY FOR TAX.—

"(A) IN GENERAL.—Except as provided in subparagraph (B), the credit allowed by subsection (a) for any taxable year shall not exceed the amount of the tax imposed by this chapter reduced by the sum of the credits allowable under a section of this part having a lower number or letter designation than this section, other than the credits allowable by sections 31, 39, and 43. For purposes of the preceding sentence, the term 'tax imposed by this chapter' shall not include any tax treated as not imposed by this chapter under the last sentence of section 53(a).

"(B) SPECIAL RULE FOR PASSTHROUGH OF CREDIT.—In the case of an individual who—

"(i) owns an interest in an unincorporated trade or business,

"(ii) is a partner in a partnership,

"(iii) is a beneficiary of an estate or trust, or

"(iv) is a shareholder in an electing small business corporation (within the meaning of section 1371(b)), the credit allowed by subsection (a) for any taxable year shall not exceed the lesser of the amount determined under subparagraph (A) for the taxable year or an amount (separately computed with respect to such person's interest in such trade or business or entity) equal to the amount of tax attributable to that portion of a person's taxable income which is allocable or apportionable to the person's interest in such trade or business or entity.

"(2) CARRYBACK AND CARRYOVER OF UNUSED CREDIT.—

"(A) ALLOWANCE OF CREDIT.—If the amount of the credit determined under this section for any taxable year exceeds the limitation provided by paragraph (1) for such taxable year (hereinafter in this paragraph referred to as the 'unused credit year'), such excess shall be—

"(i) a research credit carryback to each of the 3 taxable years preceding the unused credit year, and

"(ii) a research credit carryover to each of the 15 taxable years following the unused credit year,

and shall be added to the amount allowable as a credit by this section for such years. If any portion of such excess is a carryback to a taxable year beginning before July 1, 1981, this section shall be deemed to have been in effect for such taxable year for purposes of allowing such carryback as a credit under this section. The entire amount of the unused credit for an unused credit year shall be carried to the earliest of the 18 taxable years to which (by reason of clauses (i) and (ii)) such credit may be carried, and then to each of the other 17 taxable years to the extent that, because of the limitation contained in subparagraph (B), such unused credit may not be added for a prior taxable year to which such unused credit may be carried.

"(B) LIMITATION.—The amount of the unused credit which may be added under subparagraph (A) for any preceding or succeeding taxable year shall not exceed the amount by which the limitation provided by paragraph (1) for such taxable year exceeds the sum of—

"(i) the credit allowable under this section for such taxable year, and

"(ii) the amounts which, by reason of this paragraph, are added to the amount allowable for such taxable year and which are attributable to taxable years preceding the unused credit year."

(b) TECHNICAL AMENDMENTS RELATED TO CARRYOVER AND CARRYBACK OF CREDITS.—

(1) CARRYOVER OF CREDIT.—

(A) Subparagraph (A) of section 55(c)(4) (relating to carryover and carryback of certain credits) is amended by striking out "section 44E(e)(1)" and inserting in lieu thereof "section 44F(g)(1), 44E(e)(1)".

(B) Subsection (c) of section 381 (relating to items of the distributor or transferor corporation) is amended by adding at the end thereof the following new paragraph:

"(28) CREDIT UNDER SECTION 44F.—The acquiring corporation shall take into account (to the extent proper to carry out the purposes of this section and section 44F, and under such regulations as may be prescribed by the Secretary) the items required to be taken into account for purposes of section 44F in respect of the distributor or transferor corporation."

(C) Section 383 (relating to special limitations on unused investment credits, work incentive program credits, new employee credits, alcohol fuel credits, foreign taxes, and capital losses), as in effect for taxable years beginning after June 30, 1982, is amended—

(i) by inserting "to any unused credit of the corporation under section 44F(g)(2)," after "44E(e)(2),", and

(ii) by inserting "RESEARCH CREDITS," after "ALCOHOL FUEL CREDITS," in the section heading.

(D) Section 383 (as in effect on the day before the date of the enactment of the Tax Reform Act of 1976) is amended—

(i) by inserting "to any unused credit of the corporation which could otherwise be carried forward under section 44F(g)(2)," after "44E(e)(2),", and

(ii) by inserting "RESEARCH CREDITS," after "ALCOHOL FUEL CREDITS," in the section heading.

(E) The table of sections for part V of subchapter C of chapter 1 is amended by inserting "alcohol fuel credits, research credits," after "new employee credits," in the item relating to section 383.

(2) CARRYBACK OF CREDIT.—

(A) Subparagraph (C) of section 6511(d)(4) (defining credit carryback) is amended by striking out "and new employee credit carryback" and inserting in lieu thereof "new employee credit carryback, and research credit carryback".

(B) Section 6411 (relating to quick refunds in respect of tentative carryback adjustments) is amended—

(i) by striking out "or unused new employee credit" each place it appears and inserting in lieu thereof "unused new employee credit, or unused research credit";

(ii) by inserting "by a research credit carryback provided in section 44F(g)(2)," after "53(b)," in the first sentence of subsection (a);

(iii) by striking out "or a new employee credit carryback from" each place it appears and inserting in lieu thereof "a new employee credit carryback, or a research credit carryback from"; and

(iv) by striking out "work incentive program carryback)" and inserting in lieu thereof "work incentive program carryback, or, in the case of a research credit carryback, to an investment credit carryback, a work incentive program carryback, or a new employee credit carryback)".

(c) OTHER TECHNICAL AND CLERICAL AMENDMENTS.—

(1) Subsection (b) of section 6096 (relating to designation of income tax payments to Presidential Election Campaign Fund) is amended by striking out "and 44E" and inserting in lieu thereof "44E, and 44F".

(2) The table of sections for subpart A of part IV of subchapter A of chapter 1 is amended by inserting after the item relating to section 44E the following new item:

"Sec. 44F. Credit for increasing research activities."

(d) EFFECTIVE DATE.—

(1) IN GENERAL.—The amendments made by this section shall apply to amounts paid or incurred after June 30, 1981, and before January 1, 1986.

(2) TRANSITIONAL RULE.—

(A) IN GENERAL.—If, with respect to the first taxable year to which the amendments made by this section apply and which ends in 1981 or 1982, the taxpayer may only take into account qualified research expenses paid or incurred during a portion of such taxable year, the amount of the qualified research expenses taken into account for the base period of such taxable year shall be the amount which bears the same ratio to the total qualified research expenses for such base period as the number of months in such portion of such taxable year bears to the total number of months in such taxable year. A similar rule shall apply in the case of a taxpayer's first taxable year ending after December 31, 1985.

(B) DEFINITIONS.—For purposes of the preceding sentence, the terms "qualified research expenses" and "base period" have the meanings given to such terms by section 44F of the Internal Revenue Code of 1954 (as added by this section).

## Charitable Contributions of Scientific Property Used for Research

(Section 222)

(a) IN GENERAL.—Subsection (e) of section 170 (relating to deductions for charitable, etc., contributions and gifts) is amended by adding at the end thereof the following new paragraph:

"(4) SPECIAL RULE FOR CONTRIBUTIONS OF SCIENTIFIC PROPERTY USED FOR RESEARCH.—

"(A) LIMIT ON REDUCTION.—In the case of a qualified research contribution, the reduction under paragraph (1)(A) shall be no greater than the amount determined under paragraph (3)(B).

"(B) QUALIFIED RESEARCH CONTRIBUTIONS.—For purposes of this paragraph, the term 'qualified research contribution' means a charitable contribution by a corporation of tangible personal property described in paragraph (1) of section 1221, but only if—

"(i) the contribution is to an educational organization which is described in subsection (b)(1)(A)(ii) of this section and which is an institution of higher education (as defined in section 3304(f)),

"(ii) the property is constructed by the taxpayer,

"(iii) the contribution is made not later than 2 years after the date the construction of the property is substantially completed,

"(iv) the original use of the property is by the donee,

"(v) the property is scientific equipment or apparatus substantially all of the use of which by the donee is for research or experimentation (within the meaning of section 174), or for research training, in the United States in physical or biological sciences,

"(vi) the property is not transferred by the donee in exchange for money, other property, or services, and

"(vii) the taxpayer receives from the donee a written statement representing that its use and disposition of the property will be in accordance with the provisions of clauses (v) and (vi).

"(C) CONSTRUCTION OF PROPERTY BY TAXPAYER.—For purposes of this paragraph, property shall be treated as constructed by the taxpayer only if the cost of the parts used in the construction of such property (other than parts manufactured by the taxpayer or a related person) do not exceed 50 percent of the taxpayer's basis in such property.

"(D) CORPORATION.—For purposes of this paragraph, the term 'corporation' shall not include—

"(i) an electing small business corporation (as defined in section 1371(b)),

"(ii) a personal holding company (as defined in section 542), and

"(iii) a service organization (as defined in section 414(m)(3))."

(b) EFFECTIVE DATE.—The amendment made by subsection (a) shall apply to charitable contributions made after the date of the enactment of this Act, in taxable years ending after such date.

## Reduction in Corporate Tax Rates

(Section 231)

(a) IN GENERAL.—Subsection (b) of section 11 (relating to amount of corporate tax) is amended—

(1) by striking out "17 percent" in paragraph (1) and inserting in lieu thereof "15 percent (16 percent for taxable years beginning in 1982)", and

(2) by striking out "20 percent" in paragraph (2) and inserting in lieu thereof "18 percent (19 percent for taxable years beginning in 1982)".

(b) CONFORMING AMENDMENTS.—

(1) Paragraph (2) of section 821(a) (relating to imposition of tax on mutual insurance companies to which part II applies) is amended to read as follows:

"(2) CAP ON TAX WHERE INCOME IS LESS THAN $12,000.—The tax imposed by paragraph (1) on so much of the mutual insurance company taxable income as does not exceed $12,000 shall not exceed 32 percent (30 percent for taxable years beginning after December 31, 1982) of the amount by which such income exceeds $6,000."

(2) Subparagraph (B) of section 821(c)(1) (relating to imposition of alternative tax for certain small companies) is amended to read as follows:

"(B) CAP WHERE INCOME IS LESS THAN $6,000.—The tax imposed by subparagraph (A) on so much of the taxable investment income as does not exceed $6,000 shall not exceed 32 percent (30 percent for taxable years beginning after December 31, 1982) of the amount by which such income exceeds $3,000."

(3) The amendments made by paragraphs (1) and (2) shall apply to taxable years beginning after December 31, 1978; except that for purposes of applying sections 821(a)(2) and 821(c)(1)(B) of the Internal Revenue Code of 1954 (as amended by this subsection) to taxable years beginning before January 1, 1982, the percentage

referred to in such section shall be deemed to be 34 percent.
(c) EFFECTIVE DATE.—The amendments made by subsection (a) shall apply to taxable years beginning after December 31, 1981.

## Increase in Allowable Charitable Deduction for Corporations

(Section 263)

(a) IN GENERAL.—Paragraph (2) of section 170(b) (relating to percentage limitations) is amended by striking out "5 percent" and inserting in lieu thereof "10 percent".
(b) EFFECTIVE DATE.—The amendment made by this section shall apply to taxable years beginning after December 31, 1981.

## Partial Exclusion of Interest from Gross Income

(Section 302)

(a) AMOUNT OF EXCLUSION.—Section 128 (relating to the interest on certain savings certificates) is amended to read as follows:
"SEC. 128. PARTIAL EXCLUSION OF INTEREST.

"(a) IN GENERAL.—-Gross income does not include the amounts received during the taxable year by an individual as interest.
"(b) MAXIMUM DOLLAR AMOUNT.—The aggregate amount excludable under subsection (a) for any taxable year shall not exceed 15 percent of the lesser of—
        "(1) $3,000 ($6,000 in the case of a joint return under section 6013), or
        "(2) the excess of the amount of interest received by the taxpayer during such taxable year (less the amount of any deduction under section 62(12)) over the amount of qualified interest expenses of such taxpayer for the taxable year.
"(c) DEFINITIONS.—For purposes of this section—
    "(1) INTEREST DEFINED.—The term 'interest' means—
        "(A) interest on deposits with a bank (as defined in section 581),
        "(B) amounts (whether or not designated as interest) paid, in respect of deposits, investment certificates, or withdrawable or repurchasable shares, by—
            "(i) an institution which is—
                "(I) a mutual savings bank, cooperative bank, domestic building and loan association, or credit

union, or

"(II) any other savings or thrift institution which is chartered and supervised under Federal or State law,

the deposits or accounts in which are insured under Federal or State law or which are protected and guaranteed under State law, or

"(ii) an industrial loan association or bank chartered and supervised under Federal or State law in a manner similar to a savings and loan institution.

"(C) interest on—

"(i) evidences of indebtedness (including bonds, debentures, notes, and certificates) issued by a domestic corporation in registered form, and

"(ii) to the extent provided in regulations prescribed by the Secretary, other evidences of indebtedness issued by a domestic corporation of a type offered by corporations to the public,

"(D) interest on obligations of the United States, a State, or a political subdivision of a State (not excluded from gross income of the taxpayer under any other provision of law),

"(E) interest attributable to participation shares in a trust established and maintained by a corporation established pursuant to Federal law, and

"(F) interest paid by an insurance company under an agreement to pay interest on—

"(i) prepaid premiums,

"(ii) life insurance policy proceeds which are left on deposit with such company by a beneficiary, and

"(iii) under regulations prescribed by the Secretary, policyholder dividends left on deposit with such company.

"(2) QUALIFIED INTEREST EXPENSE DEFINED.—The term 'qualified interest expense' means an amount equal to the excess of—

"(A) the amount of the deduction allowed the taxpayer under section 163(a) (relating to interest) for the taxable year, over

"(B) the amount of such deduction allowed with respect to interest paid or accrued on indebtedness incurred in—

"(i) acquiring, constructing, reconstructing, or rehabilitating property which is primarily used by the taxpayer as a dwelling unit (as defined in section 280A(f)(1)), or

"(ii) the taxpayer's conduct of a trade or business."

(b) REPEAL OF PARTIAL EXCLUSION OF INTEREST.—

(1) IN GENERAL.—Subsection (c) of section 404 of the Crude Oil Windfall Profit Tax Act of 1980 is amended by striking out "1983" and inserting in lieu thereof "1982".

(2) CONFORMING AMENDMENT.—Section 116(a) (relating to par-

tial exclusion of dividends) is amended to read as follows:
"(a) EXCLUSION FROM GROSS INCOME.—

"(1) IN GENERAL.—Gross income does not include amounts received by an individual as dividends from domestic corporations.

"(2) MAXIMUM DOLLAR AMOUNT.—The aggregate amount excluded under subsection (a) for any taxable year shall not exceed $100 ($200 in the case of a joint return under section 6013)."

(c) CONFORMING AMENDMENTS.—

(1) The table of sections for part III of subchapter B of chapter 1, as amended by section 301(b)(1), is amended by striking out the item relating to section 128 and inserting in lieu thereof the following new item:

"Sec. 128. Partial exclusion of interest."

(2) Section 265 (relating to expenses and interest relating to tax-exempt income), as amended by section 301(b)(2), is amended by striking out "or to purchase or carry any certificate to the extent the interest on such certificate is excludable under section 128" and inserting in lieu thereof "or to purchase or carry obligations or shares, or to make other deposits or investments, the interest on which is described in section 128(c)(1) to the extent such interest is excludable from gross income under section 128".

(3) Section 46(c)(8) (relating to limitation to amount at risk) is amended by striking out "clause (i), (ii), or (iii) of subparagraph (A) or subparagraph (B) of section 128(c)(2)" and inserting in lieu thereof "subparagraph (A) or (B) of section 128(c)(1)".

(4) Subsection (b) of section 854 is amended to read as follows:

'(b) OTHER DIVIDENDS AND TAXABLE INTEREST.—

"(1) DEDUCTION UNDER SECTION 243.—In the case of a dividend received from a regulated investment company (other than a dividend to which subsection (a) applies)—

"(A) if such investment company meets the requirements of section 852(a) for the taxable year during which it paid such dividend; and

"(B) the aggregate dividends received by such company during such taxable year are less than 75 percent of its gross income.

then, in computing the deduction under section 243, there shall be taken into account only that portion of the dividend which bears the same ratio to the amount of such dividend as the aggregate dividends received by such company during such taxable year bear to its gross income for such taxable year.

"(2) EXCLUSION UNDER SECTIONS 116 AND 128.—For purposes of sections 116 and 128, in the case of any dividend (other than a dividend described in subsection (a)) received from a regulated investment company which meets the requirements of section 852 for the taxable year in which it paid the dividend—

"(A) the entire amount of such dividend shall be treated as a dividend if the aggregate dividends received by such company during the taxable year equal or exceed 75 percent of its gross income,

"(B) the entire amount of such dividend shall be treated as interest if the aggregate interest received by such company during the taxable year equals or exceeds 75 percent of its gross income, or

"(C) if subparagraphs (A) and (B) do not apply, a portion of such dividend shall be treated as a dividend (and a portion of such dividend shall be treated as interest) based on the portion of the company's gross income which consists of aggregate dividends or aggregate interest, as the case may be. For purposes of the preceding sentence, gross income and aggregate interest received shall each be reduced by so much of the deduction allowable by section 163 for the taxable year as does not exceed aggregate interest received for the taxable year.

"(3) NOTICE TO SHAREHOLDERS.—The amount of any distribution by a regulated investment company which may be taken into account as a dividend for purposes of the exclusion under section 116 and the deduction under section 243 or as interest for purposes of section 128 shall not exceed the amount so designated by the company in a written notice to its shareholders mailed not later than 45 days after the close of its taxable year.

"(4) DEFINITIONS.—For purposes of this subsection—

"(A) The term 'gross income' does not include gain from the sale or other disposition of stock or securities.

"(B) The term 'aggregate dividends received' includes only dividends received from domestic corporations other than dividends described in section 116(b)(2) (relating to dividends excluded from gross income). In determining the amount of any dividend for purposes of this subparagraph, the rules provided in section 116(c)(2) (relating to certain distributions) shall apply.

"(C) The term 'aggregate interest received' includes only interest described in section 128(c)(1)."

(5) Subsection (c) of section 857 is amended to read as follows:

"(c) LIMITATIONS APPLICABLE TO DIVIDENDS RECEIVED FROM REAL ESTATE INVESTMENT TRUSTS.—

"(1) IN GENERAL.—For purposes of section 116 (relating to an exclusion for dividends received by individuals) and section 243 (relating to deductions for dividends received by corporations), a dividend received from a real estate investment trust which meets the requirements of this part shall not be considered as a dividend.

"(2) TREATMENT FOR SECTION 128.—In the case of a dividend (other than a capital gain dividend, as defined in subsection (b)(3)(C)) received from a real estate investment trust which meets the requirements of this part for the taxable year in which it paid the dividend—

"(A) such dividend shall be treated as interest if the aggregate interest received by the real estate investment trust for the taxable year equals or exceeds 75 percent of its gross income, or

"(B) if subparagraph (A) does not apply, the portion of such dividend which bears the same ratio to the amount of such dividend as the aggregate interest received bears to gross income shall be treated as interest.

"(3) ADJUSTMENTS TO GROSS INCOME AND AGGREGATE INTEREST RECEIVED.—For purposes of paragraph (2)—

"(A) gross income does not include the net capital gain,

"(B) gross income and aggregate interest received shall each be reduced by so much of the deduction allowable by section 163 for the taxable year (other than for interest on mortgages on real property owned by the real estate investment trust) as does not exceed aggregate interest received by the taxable year, and

"(C) gross income shall be reduced by the sum of the taxes imposed by paragraphs (4), (5), and (6) of section 857(b).

"(4) AGGREGATE INTEREST RECEIVED.—For purposes of this subsection, the term 'aggregate interest received' means only interest described in section 128(c)(1).

"(5) NOTICE TO SHAREHOLDERS.—The amount of any distribution by a real estate investment trust which may be taken into account as interest for purposes of the exclusion under section 128 shall not exceed the amount so designated by the trust in a written notice to its shareholders mailed not later than 45 days after the close of its taxable year."

(d) EFFECTIVE DATES.—

(1) IN GENERAL.—The amendments made by subsections (a) and (c) shall apply to taxable years beginning after December 31, 1984.

(2) DIVIDEND EXCLUSION.—The amendment made by subsection (b)(2) shall apply to taxable years beginning after December 31, 1981.


## Increase in Estate and Gift Tax Unified Credit

(Section 401)

(a) CREDIT AGAINST ESTATE TAX.—

(1) IN GENERAL.—Subsection (a) of section 2010 (relating to unified credit against estate tax) is amended by striking out "$47,000" and inserting in lieu thereof "$192,800".

(2) CONFORMING AMENDMENTS.—
(A) Subsection (b) of section 2010 is amended to read as follows:
"(b) PHASE-IN OF CREDIT.—

| "In the case of decedents dying in: | Subsection (a) shall be applied by substituting for '$192,800' the following amount: |
|---|---|
| 1982 | $62,800 |
| 1983 | 79,300 |
| 1984 | 96,300 |
| 1985 | 121,800 |
| 1986 | 155,800." |

(B) Subsection (a) of section 6018 (relating to estate tax returns by executors) is amended—
(i) by striking out "$175,000" in paragraph (1) and inserting in lieu thereof "$600,000"; and
(ii) by striking out paragraph (3) and inserting in lieu thereof the following:

"(3) PHASE-IN OF FILING REQUIREMENT AMOUNT.—

| "In the case of decedents dying in: | Paragraph (1) shall be applied by substituting for '$600,000' the following amount: |
|---|---|
| 1982 | $225,000 |
| 1983 | 275,000 |
| 1984 | 325,000 |
| 1985 | 400,000 |
| 1986 | 500,000." |

(b) CREDIT AGAINST GIFT TAX.—
(1) IN GENERAL.—Paragraph (1) of section 2505(a) (relating to unified credit against gift tax) is amended by striking out "$47,000" and inserting in lieu thereof "$192,800".
(2) CONFORMING AMENDMENT.—Subsection (b) of section 2505 is amended to read as follows:
"(b) PHASE-IN OF CREDIT.—

| "In the case of gifts made in: | Subsection (a)(1) shall be applied by substituting for '$192,800' the following amount: |
|---|---|
| 1982 | $62,800 |
| 1983 | 79,300 |
| 1984 | 96,300 |
| 1985 | 121,800 |
| 1986 | 155,800." |

# Reduction in Maximum Estate and Gift Tax Rates

(Section 402)

(a) 50 PERCENT MAXIMUM RATE.—Subsection (c) of section 2001 (relating to rate schedule) is amended by striking out the item beginning "Over $2,500,000" and all that follows and inserting in lieu thereof the following new item:

"Over $2,500,000 ........................................    $1,025,800, plus 50% of the excess over $2,500,000."

(b) PHASE-IN OF 50 PERCENT MAXIMUM RATE.—Subsection (c) of section 2001 is amended—

(1) by striking out "(c) RATE SCHEDULE.—" and inserting in lieu thereof the following:

"(c) RATE SCHEDULE.—

"(1) IN GENERAL.—", and

(2) by adding at the end thereof the following new paragraph:

"(2) PHASE-IN OF 50 PERCENT MAXIMUM RATE.—

"(A) IN GENERAL.—In the case of decedents dying, and gifts made, before 1985, there shall be substituted for the last item in the schedule contained in paragraph (1) the items determined under this paragraph.

"(B) FOR 1982.—In the case of decedents dying, and gifts made, in 1982, the substitution under this paragraph shall be as follows:

"Over $2,500,000 but not over $3,000,000 .    $1,025,800, plus 53% of the excess over $2,500,000.

Over $3,000,000 but not over $3,500,000 ...    $1,290,800, plus 57% of the excess over $3,000,000.

Over $3,500,000 but not over $4,000,000 ...    $1,575,800, plus 61% of the excess over $3,500,000.

Over $4,000,000 ..........................................    $1,880,800, plus 65% of the excess over $4,000,000.

"(C) FOR 1983.—In the case of decedents dying, and gifts made, in 1983, the substitution under this paragraph shall be as follows:

"Over $2,500,000 but not over $3,000,000 .    $1,025,800, plus 53% of the excess over $2,500,000.

Over $3,000,000 but not over $3,500,000 ...    $1,290,800, plus 57% of the excess over $3,000,000.

Over $3,500,000 ..........................................    $1,575,800, plus 60% of the excess over $3,500,000.

"(D) FOR 1984.—In the case of decedents dying, and gifts made, in 1984, the substitution under this paragraph shall be as follows:

"Over $2,500,000 but not over $3,000,000 .    $1,025,800, plus 53% of the excess over $2,500,000.

Over $3,000,000 ..........................................    $1,290,800, plus 55% of the excess over $3,000,000."

(c) ADJUSTMENT IN COMPUTATION OF TAX FOR GIFTS MADE AFTER DECEMBER 31, 1976.—Paragraph (2) of section 2001(b) is amended to read as follows:

"(2) the aggregate amount of tax which would have been payable under chapter 12 with respect to gifts made by the decedent after December 31, 1976, if the rate schedule set forth in subsection (c) (as in effect at the decedent's death) had been applicable at the time of such gifts."

# Unlimited Marital Deductions

(Section 403)

(a) ESTATE TAX DEDUCTION.—

(1) IN GENERAL.—Section 2056 (relating to bequests, etc., to surviving spouses) is amended—

(A) by striking out subsection (c) and redesignating subsection (d) as subsection (c); and

(B) by striking out "subsections (b) and (c)" in subsection (a) and inserting in lieu thereof "subsection (b)".

(2) CONFORMING AMENDMENTS.—

(A) Paragraph (2) of section 2012(b) (relating to credit for gift tax) is amended to read as follows:

"(2) if a deduction with respect to such gift is allowed under section 2056(a) (relating to marital deduction), then by the amount of such value, reduced as provided in paragraph (1); and".

(B) Paragraph (5) of section 2602(c) (relating to coordination with estate tax) is amended by striking out subparagraph (A) and redesignating subparagraphs (B) and (C) as subparagraphs (A) and (B), respectively.

(C) Subparagraph (A) of section 691(c)(3) (relating to special rules for generation-skipping transfers) is amended by striking out "section 2602(c)(5)(C)" and inserting in lieu thereof "section 2602(c)(5)(B)".

(b) GIFT TAX DEDUCTION.—

(1) IN GENERAL.—Subsection (a) of section 2523 (relating to gift to spouse) is amended to read as follows:

"(a) ALLOWANCE OF DEDUCTION.—Where a donor who is a citizen or resident transfers during the calendar year by gift an interest in property to a donee who at the time of the gift is the donor's spouse, there shall be allowed as a deduction in computing taxable gifts for the calendar year an amount with respect to such interest equal to its value."

(2) TECHNICAL AMENDMENT.—Section 2523 is amended by striking out subsection (f).

(3) CONFORMING AMENDMENTS.—

(A) So much of section 6019 (relating to gift tax returns) as follows the heading and precedes subsection (b) is amended to read as follows:

"Any individual who in any calendar year makes any transfer by gift other than—

"(1) a transfer which under subsection (b) or (e) of section 2503 is not to be included in the total amount of gifts for such year, or

"(2) a transfer of an interest with respect to which a deduction is allowed under section 2523, shall make a return for such year with respect to the gift tax imposed by subtitle B."

(B) Paragraph (2) of section 2035(b) is amended by inserting "(other than by reason of section 6019(a)(2))" after "section 6019".

(c) ESTATE TAX ON PROPERTY HELD JOINTLY BY HUSBAND AND WIFE.

(1) IN GENERAL.—Paragraph (2) of section 2040(b) (defining qualified joint interest) is amended to read as follows:

"(2) QUALIFIED JOINT INTEREST DEFINED.—For purposes of paragraph (1), the term 'qualified joint interest' means any interest in property held by the decedent and the decedent's spouse as—

"(A) tenants by the entirety, or

"(B) joint tenants with right of survivorship, but only if the decedent and the spouse of the decedent are the only joint tenants."

(2) TECHNICAL AMENDMENT.—Subsection (a) of section 2040 is amended by striking out "joint tenants" each place it appears and inserting in lieu thereof "joint tenants with right of survivorship".

(3) CONFORMING AMENDMENTS.—

(A) Subsections (c), (d), and (e) of section 2040 are hereby repealed.

(B) Section 2515 (relating to tenancies by the entirety in real property), section 2515A (relating to tenancies by the entirety in personal property), and subsection (c) of section 6019 (relating to gift tax return) are hereby repealed.

(C) The table of sections for subchapter B of chapter 12 (relating to transfers) is amended by striking out the items relating to sections 2515 and 2515A.

(d) ELECTION TO HAVE CERTAIN LIFE INTERESTS QUALIFY FOR MARITAL DEDUCTION.—

(1) ESTATE TAX.—Subsection (b) of section 2056 is amended by adding at the end thereof the following new paragraphs:

"(7) ELECTION WITH RESPECT TO LIFE ESTATE FOR SURVIVING SPOUSE.—

"(A) IN GENERAL.—In the case of qualified terminable interest property—

"(i) for purposes of subsection (a), such property shall be treated as passing to the surviving spouse, and

"(ii) for purposes of paragraph (1)(A), no part of such property shall be treated as passing to any person other than the surviving spouse.

"(B) QUALIFIED TERMINABLE INTEREST PROPERTY DEFINED.—For purposes of this paragraph—

"(i) IN GENERAL.—The term 'qualified terminable interest property' means property—

"(I) which passes from the decedent,

"(II) in which the surviving spouse has a qualifying income interest for life, and

"(III) to which an election under this paragraph applies.

"(ii) QUALIFYING INCOME INTEREST FOR LIFE.—The surviving spouse has a qualifying income interest for life if—

"(I) the surviving spouse is entitled to all the income from the property, payable annually or at more frequent intervals, and

"(II) no person has a power to appoint any part of the property to any person other than the surviving spouse.

Subclause (II) shall not apply to a power exercisable only at or after the death of the surviving spouse.

"(iii) PROPERTY INCLUDES INTEREST THEREIN.—The term 'property' includes an interest in property.

"(iv) SPECIFIC PORTION TREATED AS SEPARATE PROPERTY.—A specific portion of property shall be treated as separate property.

"(v) ELECTION.—An election under this paragraph with respect to any property shall be made by the executor on the return of tax imposed by section 2001. Such an election, once made, shall be irrevocable.

"(8) SPECIAL RULE FOR CHARITABLE REMAINDER TRUSTS.—

"(A) IN GENERAL.—If the surviving spouse of the decedent is the only noncharitable beneficiary of a qualified charitable remainder trust, paragraph (1) shall not apply to any interest in such trust which passes or has passed from the decedent to such surviving spouse.

"(B) DEFINITIONS.—For purposes of subparagraph (A)—

"(i) NONCHARITABLE BENEFICIARY.—The term 'noncharitable beneficiary' means any beneficiary of the qualified charitable remainder trust other than an organization described in section 170(c).

"(ii) QUALIFIED CHARITABLE REMAINDER TRUST.—The term 'qualified charitable remainder trust' means a charitable remainder annuity trust or charitable remainder unitrust (described in section 664)."

(2) GIFT TAX.—Section 2523 is amended by adding at the end thereof the following new subsections:

"(f) ELECTION WITH RESPECT TO LIFE ESTATE FOR DONEE SPOUSE.—

"(1) IN GENERAL.—In the case of qualified terminable interest property—

"(A) for purposes of subsection (a), such property shall be treated as transferred to the donee spouse, and

"(B) for purposes of subsection (b)(1), no part of such property shall be considered as retained in the donor or transferred to any person other than the donee spouse.

"(2) QUALIFIED TERMINABLE INTEREST PROPERTY.—For purposes of this subsection, the term 'qualified terminable interest property' means any property—

"(A) which is transferred by the donor spouse,

"(B) in which the donee spouse has a qualifying income interest for life, and

"(C) to which an election under this subsection applies.

"(3) CERTAIN RULES MADE APPLICABLE.—For purposes of this subsection, the rules of clauses (ii), (iii), and (iv) of section 2056(b)(7)(B) shall apply.

"(4) ELECTION.—An election under this subsection with respect to any property shall be made on the return of the tax imposed by section 2501 for the calendar year in which the interest was transferred. Such an election, once made, shall be irrevocable.

"(g) SPECIAL RULE FOR CHARITABLE REMAINDER TRUSTS.—

"(1) IN GENERAL.—If, after the transfer, the donee spouse is the only noncharitable beneficiary (other than the donor) of a qualified remainder trust, subsection (b) shall not apply to the interest in such trust which is transferred to the donee spouse.

"(2) DEFINITIONS.—For purposes of paragraph (1), the term 'noncharitable beneficiary' and 'qualified charitable remainder trust' have the meanings given to such terms by section 2056(b)(8)(B)."

(3) TREATMENT OF SPOUSE.—

(A) INCLUSION IN GROSS ESTATE.—

(i) IN GENERAL.—Part III of subchapter A of chapter 11 is amended by redesignating sections 2044 and 2045 as sections 2045 and 2046, respectively, and by inserting after section 2043 the following new section:

"SEC. 2044. CERTAIN PROPERTY FOR WHICH MARITAL DEDUCTION WAS PREVIOUSLY ALLOWED.

"(a) GENERAL RULE.—The value of the gross estate shall include the value of any property to which this section applies in which the decedent had a qualifying income interest for life.

"(b) PROPERTY TO WHICH THIS SECTION APPLIES.—This section applies to any property if—

"(1) a deduction was allowed with respect to the transfer of such property to the decedent—

"(A) under section 2056 by reason of subsection (b)(7) thereof, or

"(B) under section 2523 by reason of subsection (f) thereof, and

"(2) section 2519 (relating to dispositions of certain life estates) did not apply with respect to a disposition by the decedent of part or all of such property."

(ii) The table of sections for part III of subchapter A of chapter 11 is amended by redesignating the items relating to sections 2044 and 2045 as sections 2045 and 2046, respectively, and by inserting after the item relating to section 2043 the following new item:

"Sec. 2044. Certain property for which marital deduction was previously allowed."

(B) GIFT TAX.—

(i) IN GENERAL.—Subchapter B of chapter 11 (relating to transfers) is amended by adding at the end thereof the following new section:

"SEC. 2519. DISPOSITIONS OF CERTAIN LIFE ESTATES.

"(a) GENERAL RULE.—Any disposition of all or part of a qualifying income interest for life in any property to which this section applies shall be treated as a transfer of such property.

"(b) PROPERTY TO WHICH THIS SUBSECTION APPLIES.—This section applies to any property if a deduction was allowed with respect to the transfer of such property to the donor—

"(1) under section 2056 by reason of subsection (b)(7) thereof, or

"(2) under section 2523 by reason of subsection (f) thereof."

(ii) The table of sections for subchapter B of chapter 11 is amended by adding at the end thereof the following new item:

"Sec. 2519. Dispositions of certain life estates."

(4)(A) Subchapter C of chapter 11 is amended by inserting after section 2207 the following new section:

"SEC. 2207A. RIGHT OF RECOVERY IN THE CASE OF CERTAIN MARITAL DEDUCTION PROPERTY.

"(a) RECOVERY WITH RESPECT TO ESTATE TAX.—

"(1) IN GENERAL.—If any part of the gross estate consists of property the value of which is includible in the gross estate by reason of section 2044 (relating to certain property for which marital deduction was previously allowed), the decedent's estate shall be entitled to recover from the person receiving the property the amount by which—

"(A) the total tax under this chapter which has been paid, exceeds

"(B) the total tax under this chapter which would have been payable if the value of such property had not been included in the gross estate.

"(2) DECEDENT MAY OTHERWISE DIRECT BY WILL.—Paragraph (1) shall not apply if the decedent otherwise directs by will.

"(b) RECOVERY WITH RESPECT TO GIFT TAX.—If for any calendar year tax is paid under chapter 12 with respect to any person by reason of property treated as transferred by such person under section 2519, such person shall be entitled to recover from the person receiving the property the amount by which—

"(1) the total tax for such year under chapter 12, exceeds

"(2) the total tax which would have been payable under such chapter for such year if the value of such property had not been taken into account for purposes of chapter 12.

"(c) MORE THAN ONE RECIPIENT OF PROPERTY.—For purposes of this section, if there is more than one person receiving the property, the right of recovery shall be against each such person.

"(d) TAXES AND INTEREST.—In the case of penalties and interest attributable to additional taxes described in subsections (a) and (b), rules similar to subsections (a), (b), and (c) shall apply."

(B) The table of sections for subchapter C of chapter 11 is amended by inserting after the item relating to section 2207 the following new item:

"Sec. 2207A. Right of recovery in the case of certain marital deduction property."

(e) EFFECTIVE DATES.—

(1) Except as otherwise provided in this subsection, the amendments made by this section shall apply to the estates of decedents dying after December 31, 1981.

(2) The amendments made by paragraphs (1), (2), and (3)(A) of subsection (b), subparagraphs (B) and (C) of subsection (c)(3), and paragraphs (2) and (3)(B) of subsection (d) shall apply to gifts made after December 31, 1981.

(3) If—

(A) the decedent dies after December 31, 1981,

(B) by reason of the death of the decedent property passes from the decedent or is acquired from the decedent under a will executed before the date which is 30 days after the date of the enactment of this Act, or a trust created before such date, which contains a formula expressly providing that the spouse is to receive the maximum amount of property qualifying for the marital deduction allowable by Federal law,

(C) the formula referred to in subparagraph (B) was not amended to refer specifically to an unlimited marital deduction at any time after the date which is 30 days after the date of enactment of this Act, and before the death of the decedent, and

(D) the State does not enact a statute applicable to such estate which construes this type of formula as referring to the marital deduction allowable by Federal law as amended by subsection (a),

then the amendment made by subsection (a) shall not apply to the estate of such decedent.

# Valuation of Certain Farms, etc., Real Property

(Section 421)

(a) INCREASE IN LIMITATION.—Paragraph (2) of section 2032A(a) (relating to limitation) is amended to read as follows:

"(2) LIMIT ON AGGREGATE REDUCTION IN FAIR MARKET VALUE.— The aggregate decrease in the value of qualified real property taken into account for purposes of this chapter which results from the application of paragraph (1) with respect to any decedent shall not exceed the applicable limit set forth in the following table:

| "In the case of decedents dying in: | The applicable limit is: |
|---|---|
| 1981 | $600,000 |
| 1982 | 700,000 |
| 1983 or thereafter | 750,000." |

(b) DEFINITION OF QUALIFIED REAL PROPERTY.—

(1) REQUIRED USE CAN BE BY MEMBER OF FAMILY.—Paragraph (1) of section 2032A(b) (defining qualified real property) is amended by inserting "by the decedent or a member of the decedent's family" after "qualified use" each place it appears.

(2) SPECIAL RULES FOR DECEDENTS WHO ARE RETIRED OR DISABLED AND FOR SURVIVING SPOUSES.—Subsection (b) of section 2032A is amended by adding at the end thereof the following new paragraphs:

"(4) DECEDENTS WHO ARE RETIRED OR DISABLED.—

"(A) IN GENERAL.—If, on the date of the decedent's death, the requirements of paragraph (1)(C)(ii) with respect to the decedent for any property are not met, and the decedent—

"(i) was receiving old-age benefits under title II of the Social Security Act for a continuous period ending on such date, or

"(ii) was disabled for a continuous period ending on such date,

then paragraph (1)(C)(ii) shall be applied with respect to such property by substituting 'the date on which the longer of such continuous periods began' for 'the date of the decedent's death' in paragraph (1)(C).

"(B) DISABLED DEFINED.—For purposes of subparagraph (A), an individual shall be disabled if such individual has a mental or physical impairment which renders him unable to materially participate in the operation of the farm or other business.

"(C) COORDINATION WITH RECAPTURE.—For purposes of subsection (c)(6)(B)(i), if the requirements of paragraph (1)(C)(ii) are met with respect to any decedent by reason of subparagraph (A), the period ending on the date on which the continuous period taken into account under subparagraph (A) began shall be treated as the period immediately before the decedent's death.

"(5) SPECIAL RULES FOR SURVIVING SPOUSES.—

"(A) IN GENERAL.—If property is qualified real property with respect to a decedent (hereinafter in this paragraph referred to as the 'first decedent') and such property was acquired from or passed from the first decedent to the surviving spouse of the first decedent, for purposes of applying this subsection and subsection (c) in the case of the estate of such surviving spouse, active management of the farm or other business by the surviving spouse shall be treated as material participation by such surviving spouse in the operation of such farm or business.

"(B) SPECIAL RULE.—For the purposes of subparagraph (A), the determination of whether property is qualified real property with respect to the first decedent shall be made without regard to subparagraph (D) of paragraph (1) and without regard to whether an election under this section was made."

(c) DISPOSITIONS AND FAILURES TO USE FOR QUALIFIED USE.—

(1) 10-YEAR RECAPTURE PERIOD.—

(A) IN GENERAL.—Paragraph (1) of section 2032A(c) (relating to tax treatment of dispositions and failures to use for qualified use) is amended by striking out "15 years" and inserting in lieu thereof "10 years".

(B) CONFORMING AMENDMENTS.—

(i) Subsection (c) of section 2032A is amended by striking out paragraph (3) and redesignating paragraphs (4) through (7) as paragraphs (3) through (6), respectively.

(ii) Subparagraph (A) of paragraph (2) of section 2032A(h) (relating to treatment of replacement property) is amended by striking out all that follows "involuntarily converted" and inserting in lieu thereof the following: "; except that with respect to such qualified replacement property the 10-year period under paragraph (1) of subsection (c) shall be extended by any period, beyond the 2-year period referred to in section 1033(a)(2)(B)(i), during which the qualified heir was allowed to replace the qualified real property,".

(iii) Subparagraph (C) of such paragraph (2) is amended by striking out "(7)" and inserting in lieu thereof "(6)".

(2) CESSATION OF QUALIFIED USE.—

(A) IN GENERAL.—Subsection (c) of section 2032A is amended by adding at the end thereof the following new paragraph:

"(7) SPECIAL RULES.—

"(A) No TAX IF USE BEGINS WITHIN 2 YEARS.—If the date on which the qualified heir begins to use the qualified real property (hereinafter in this subparagraph referred to as the commencement date) is before the date 2 years after the decedent's death—

"(i) no tax shall be imposed under paragraph (1) by reason of the failure by the qualified heir to so use such property before the commencement date, and

"(ii) the 10-year period under paragraph (1) shall be extended by the period after the decedent's death and before the commencement date.

"(B) ACTIVE MANAGEMENT BY ELIGIBLE QUALIFIED HEIR TREATED AS MATERIAL PARTICIPATION.—For purposes of paragraph (6)(B)(ii), the active management of a farm or other business by—

"(i) an eligible qualified heir, or

"(ii) a fiduciary of an eligible qualified heir described in clause (ii) or (iii) of subparagraph (C),

shall be treated as material participation by such eligible qualified heir in the operation of such farm or business. In the case of an eligible qualified heir described in clause (ii), (iii), or (iv) of subparagraph (C), the preceding sentence shall apply only during periods during which such heir meets the requirements of such clause.

"(C) ELIGIBLE QUALIFIED HEIR.—For purposes of this paragraph, the term 'eligible qualified heir' means a qualified heir who—

"(i) is the surviving spouse of the decedent,

"(ii) has not attained the age of 21,

"(iii) is disabled (within the meaning of subsection (b)(4)(B)), or

"(iv) is a student.

"(D) STUDENT.—For purposes of subparagraph (C), an individual shall be treated as a student with respect to periods during any calendar year if (and only if) such individual is a student (within the meaning of section 151(e)(4)) for such calendar year."

(B) CONFORMING AMENDMENTS.—

(i) Subsection (e) of section 2032A (relating to definitions and special rules) is amended by adding at the end thereof the following new paragraph:

"(12) ACTIVE MANAGEMENT.—The term 'active management' means the making of the management decisions of a business (other than the daily operating decisions)."

(ii) Paragraph (6) of section 2032A(c) (as redesignated by paragraph (1)) is amended by striking out "3 years or more" and inserting in lieu thereof "more than 3 years".

(d) EXCHANGE OF QUALIFIED REAL PROPERTY.—

(1) IN GENERAL.—Section 2032A (relating to valuation of certain farm, etc., real property) is amended by adding at the end thereof the following new subsection:

"(i) EXCHANGES OF QUALIFIED REAL PROPERTY.—

"(1) TREATMENT OF PROPERTY EXCHANGED.—

"(A) EXCHANGES SOLELY FOR QUALIFIED EXCHANGE PROPERTY.—If an interest in qualified real property is exchanged solely for an interest in qualified exchange property in a transaction which qualifies under section 1031, no tax shall be imposed by subsection (c) by reason of such exchange.

"(B) EXCHANGES WHERE OTHER PROPERTY RECEIVED.—If an interest in qualified real property is exchanged for an interest in qualified exchange property and other property in a transaction which qualifies under section 1031, the amount of the tax imposed by subsection (c) by reason of such exchange shall be the amount of tax which (but for this subparagraph) would have been imposed on such exchange under subsection (c)(1), reduced by an amount which—

"(i) bears the same ratio to such tax, as

"(ii) the fair market value of the other property bears to the fair market value of the qualified real property exchanged.

For purposes of clause (ii) of the preceding sentence, fair market value shall be determined as of the time of the exchange.

"(2) TREATMENT OF QUALIFIED EXCHANGE PROPERTY.—For purposes of subsection (c)—

"(A) any interest in qualified exchange property shall be treated in the same manner as if it were a portion of the interest in qualified real property which was exchanged,

"(B) any tax imposed by subsection (c) by reason of the exchange shall be treated as a tax imposed on a partial disposition, and

"(C) paragraph (6) of subsection (c) shall be applied by treating material participation with respect to the exchanged property as material participation with respect to the qualified exchange property.

"(3) QUALIFIED EXCHANGE PROPERTY.—For purposes of this subsection, the term 'qualified exchange property' means real property which is to be used for the qualified use set forth in subparagraph (A), (B), or (C) of subsection (b)(2) under which the real property exchanged therefor originally qualified under subsection (a)."

(2) CONFORMING AMENDMENTS.—

(A) Paragraph (1) of section 2032A(f) (relating to statute of limitations) is amended—

(i) by inserting "or exchange" after "conversion",

(ii) by inserting "or (i)" after "(h)", and

(iii) by inserting "or of the exchange of property" after "replace".

(B) Paragraph (2) of section 6324B(c) (relating to special liens) is amended by inserting "and qualified exchange property (within the meaning of section 2032A(i)(3))" before the period at the end thereof.

(e) ELECTION REQUIREMENT OF SPECIAL RULES FOR INVOLUNTARY CONVERSIONS REPEALED.—

(1) IN GENERAL.—Section 2032A(h) (relating to special rules for involuntary conversions of qualified real property) is amended—

(A) by striking out "and the qualified heir makes an election under this subsection" in paragraph (1)(A); and

(B) by striking out paragraph (5).

(2) CONFORMING AMENDMENT.—Paragraph (1) of section 2032A(f) is amended by striking out "to which an election under subsection (h)" and inserting in lieu thereof "to which subsection (h)".

(f) METHOD OF VALUING FARMS.—

(1) Paragraph (7) of section 2032A(e) (relating to method of valuing farms) is amended by redesignating subparagraph (B) as subparagraph (C) and by inserting after subparagraph (A) the following new subparagraph:

"(B) VALUE BASED ON NET SHARE RENTAL IN CERTAIN CASES.—

"(i) IN GENERAL.—If there is no comparable land from which the average annual gross cash rental may be determined but there is comparable land from which the average net share rental may be determined, subparagraph (A)(i) shall be applied by substituting 'average annual net share rental' for 'average annual gross cash rental'.

"(ii) NET SHARE RENTAL.—For purposes of this paragraph, the term 'net share rental' means the excess of—

"(I) the value of the produce received by the lessor of the land on which such produce is grown, over

"(II) the cash operating expenses of growing such produce which, under the lease, are paid by the lessor."

(2) Subparagraph (C) of section 2032A(e)(7) (as redesignated by paragraph (1)) is amended by inserting after "determined" the following: "and that there is no comparable land from which the average net share rental may be determined".

(g) BASIS INCREASE WHERE RECAPTURE.—Subsection (c) of section 1016 (relating to adjustments to basis) is amended to read as follows:

"(c) INCREASE IN BASIS OF PROPERTY ON WHICH ADDITIONAL ESTATE TAX IS IMPOSED.—

"(1) TAX IMPOSED WITH RESPECT TO ENTIRE INTEREST.—If an additional estate tax is imposed under section 2032A(c)(1) with respect to any interest in property and the qualified heir makes an election under this subsection with respect to the imposition of such tax, the adjusted basis of such interest shall be increased by an amount equal to the excess of—

"(A) the fair market value of such interest on the date of the decedent's death (or the alternate valuation date under section 2032, if the executor of the decedent's estate elected the application of such section), over

"(B) the value of such interest determined under section 2032A(a).

"(2) PARTIAL DISPOSITIONS.—

"(A) IN GENERAL.—In the case of any partial disposition for which an election under this subsection is made, the increase in basis under paragraph (1) shall be an amount—

"(i) which bears the same ratio to the increase which would be determined under paragraph (1) (without regard to this paragraph) with respect to the entire interest, as

"(ii) the amount of the tax imposed under section 2032A(c)(1) with respect to such disposition bears to the adjusted tax difference attributable to the entire interest (as determined under section 2032A(c)(2)(B)).

"(B) PARTIAL DISPOSITION.—For purposes of subparagraph (A), the term 'partial disposition' means any disposition or cessation to which subsection (c)(2)(D), (h)(1)(B), or (i)(1)(B) of section 2032A applies.

"(3) TIME ADJUSTMENT MADE.—Any increase in basis under this subsection shall be deemed to have occurred immediately before the disposition or cessation resulting in the imposition of the tax under section 2032A(c)(1).

"(4) SPECIAL RULE IN THE CASE OF SUBSTITUTED PROPERTY.—If the tax under section 2032A(c)(1) is imposed with respect to qualified replacement property (as defined in section 2032A(h)(3)(B)) or qualified exchange property (as defined in section 2032A(i)(3)), the increase in basis under paragraph (1) shall be made by reference to the property involuntarily converted or exchanged (as the case may be).

"(5) ELECTION.—

"(A) IN GENERAL.—An election under this subsection shall be made at such time and in such manner as the Secretary shall by regulations prescribe. Such an election, once made, shall be irrevocable.

"(B) INTEREST ON RECAPTURED AMOUNT.—If an election is made under this subsection with respect to any additional estate tax imposed under section 2032A(c)(1), for purposes of section 6601 (relating to interest on underpayments), the last date prescribed for payment of such tax shall be deemed to be the last date prescribed for payment of the tax imposed by section 2001 with respect to the estate of the decedent (as determined for purposes of section 6601)."

(h) SPECIAL RULES FOR WOODLANDS.—

(1) VALUE OF TIMBER INCLUDED IN VALUATION; ACTIVE MANAGEMENT TREATED AS MATERIAL PARTICIPATION.—Subsection (e) of section 2032A is amended by adding at the end thereof the following new paragraph:

"(13) SPECIAL RULES FOR WOODLANDS.—

"(A) IN GENERAL.—In the case of any qualified woodland with respect to which the executor elects to have this subparagraph apply, trees growing on such woodland shall not be treated as a crop.

"(B) QUALIFIED WOODLAND.—The term 'qualified woodland' means any real property which—

"(i) is used in timber operations, and

"(ii) is an identifiable area of land such as an acre or other area for which records are normally maintained in conducting timber operations.

"(C) TIMBER OPERATIONS.—The term 'timber operations' means—

"(i) the planting, cultivating, caring for, or cutting of trees, or

"(ii) the preparation (other than milling) of trees for market.

"(D) ELECTION.—An election under subparagraph (A) shall be made on the return of the tax imposed by section 2001. Such election shall be made in such manner as the Secretary shall by regulations prescribe. Such an election, once made, shall be irrevocable."

(2) RECAPTURE UPON DISPOSITION OF TIMBER.—Paragraph (2) of section 2032A(c) (relating to amount of additional tax) is amended by adding at the end thereof the following new subparagraph:

"(E) SPECIAL RULE FOR DISPOSITION OF TIMBER.—In the case of qualified woodland to which an election under subsection (e)(13)(A) applies, if the qualified heir disposes of (or severs) any standing timber on such qualified woodland—

"(i) such disposition (or severance) shall be treated as a disposition of a portion of the interest of the qualified heir in such property, and

"(ii) the amount of the additional tax imposed by paragraph (1) with respect to such disposition shall be an amount equal to the lesser of—

"(I) the amount realized on such disposition (or, in any case other than a sale or exchange at arm's length, the fair market value of the portion of the interest disposed or severed), or

"(II) the amount of additional tax determined under this paragraph (without regard to this subparagraph) if the entire interest of the qualified heir in the qualified woodland had been disposed of, less the sum of the amount of the additional tax imposed with respect to all prior transactions involving such woodland to which this subparagraph applied.

For purposes of the preceding sentence, the disposition of a right to sever shall be treated as the disposition of the standing timber. The amount of additional tax imposed under paragraph (1) in any case in which a qualified heir disposes of his entire interest in the qualified woodland shall be reduced by any amount determined under this subparagraph with respect to such woodland."

(i) DEFINITION OF FAMILY MEMBER.—Paragraph (2) of section 2032A(e) (defining member of family) is amended to read as follows:

"(2) MEMBER OF FAMILY.—The term 'member of the family' means, with respect to any individual, only—

"(A) an ancestor of such individual,

"(B) the spouse of such individual,

"(C) a lineal descendant of such individual, of such individual's spouse, or of a parent of such individual, or

"(D) the spouse of any lineal descendant described in subparagraph (C).

For purposes of the preceding sentence, a legally adopted child of an individual shall be treated as the child of such individual by blood."

(j) MISCELLANEOUS AMENDMENTS.—

(1) PROPERTY TRANSFERRED TO CERTAIN DISCRETIONARY TRUSTS.—Subsection (g) of section 2032A (relating to application of section 2032A and section 6324B to interests in partnerships, corporations, and trusts) is amended by adding at the end thereof the following new sentence: "For purposes of the preceding sentence, an interest in a discretionary trust all the beneficiaries of which are qualified heirs shall be treated as a present interest."

(2) PROPERTY PURCHASED FROM DECEDENT'S ESTATE ELIGIBLE FOR SPECIAL VALUATION.—

(A) IN GENERAL.—Paragraph (9) of section 2032A(e) is amended by striking out subparagraphs (B) and (C) and inserting in lieu thereof the following:

"(B) such property is acquired by any person from the estate, or

"(C) such property is acquired by any person from a trust (to the extent such property is includible in the gross estate of the decedent)."

(B) NONRECOGNITION OF GAIN.—The section heading and subsections (a) and (b) of section 1040 are amended to read as follows:

"SEC. 1040. TRANSFER OF CERTAIN FARM, ETC., REAL PROPERTY.

"(a) GENERAL RULE.—If the executor of the estate of any decedent transfers to a qualified heir (within the meaning of section 2032A(e)(1)) any property with respect to which an election was made under section 2032A, then gain on such transfer shall be recognized to the estate only to the extent that, on the date of such exchange, the fair market value of such property exceeds the value of such property for purposes of chapter 11 (determined without regard to section 2032A).

"(b) SIMILAR RULE FOR CERTAIN TRUSTS.—To the extent provided in regulations prescribed by the Secretary, a rule similar to the rule provided in subsection (a) shall apply where the trustee of a trust (any portion of which is included in the gross estate of the decedent) transfers property with respect to which an election was made under section 2032A."

(C) CLERICAL AMENDMENT.—The table of sections for part III of subchapter O of chapter 1 is amended by striking out the item relating to section 1040 and inserting in lieu thereof the following:

"Sec. 1040. Transfer of certain farm, etc., real property."

(3) ELECTION MAY BE MADE ON LATE RETURNS.—Paragraph (1) of section 2032A(d) (relating to election) is amended to read as follows:

"(1) ELECTION.—The election under this section shall be made on the return of the tax imposed by section 2001. Such election shall be made in such manner as the Secretary shall by regulations prescribe. Such an election, once made, shall be irrevocable."

(4) TREATMENT OF REPLACEMENT PROPERTY.—Subsection (e) of section 2032A is amended by adding at the end thereof the following new paragraph:

"(14) TREATMENT OF REPLACEMENT PROPERTY ACQUIRED IN SECTION 1031 OR 1033 TRANSACTIONS.—

"(A) IN GENERAL.—In the case of any qualified replacement property, any period during which there was ownership, qualified use, or material participation with respect to the replaced property by the decedent or any member of his family shall be treated as a period during which there was such ownership, use, or material participation (as the case may be) with respect to the qualified replacement property.

"(B) LIMITATION.—Subparagraph (A) shall not apply to the extent that the fair market value of the qualified replacement property (as of the date of its acquisition) exceeds the fair market value of the replaced property (as of the date of its disposition).

"(C) DEFINITIONS.—For purposes of this paragraph—

"(i) QUALIFIED REPLACEMENT PROPERTY.—The term

'qualified replacement property' means any real property which is—
"(I) acquired in an exchange which qualifies under section 1031, or
"(II) the acquisition of which results in the non-recognition of gain under section 1033.
Such term shall only include property which is used for the same qualified use as the replaced property was being used before the exchange.
"(ii) REPLACED PROPERTY.—The term 'replaced property' means—
"(I) the property transferred in the exchange which qualifies under section 1031, or
"(II) the property compulsorily or involuntarily converted (within the meaning of section 1033)."

(k) EFFECTIVE DATES.—

(1) IN GENERAL.—Except as otherwise provided in this subsection, the amendments made by this section shall apply with respect to the estates of decedents dying after December 31, 1981.

(2) INCREASE IN LIMITATION.—The amendment made by subsection (a) shall apply with respect to the estates of decedents dying after December 31, 1980.

(3) SUBSECTION (d).—The amendments made by subsection (d) shall apply with respect to exchanges after December 31, 1981.

(4) SUBSECTION (e).—The amendments made by subsection (e) shall apply with respect to involuntary conversions after December 31, 1981.

(5) CERTAIN AMENDMENTS MADE RETROACTIVE TO 1976.—

(A) IN GENERAL.—The amendments made by subsections (b)(1), (c)(2), (j)(1), and (j)(2) shall apply with respect to the estates of decedents dying after December 31, 1976.

(B) TIMELY ELECTION REQUIRED.—Subparagraph (A) shall only apply in the case of an estate if a timely election under section 2032A was made with respect to such estate. If the time for making an election under section 2032A with respect to any estate would have otherwise expired after July 28, 1980, the time for making such election shall not expire before the date 6 months after the date of the enactment of this Act.

(C) REINSTATEMENT OF ELECTIONS.—If any election under section 2032A was revoked before the date of the enactment of this Act, such election may be reinstated within 6 months after the date of the enactment of this Act.

(D) STATUTE OF LIMITATIONS.—If on the date of the enactment of this Act (or at any time within 6 months after such date of enactment) the making of a credit or refund of any overpayment of tax resulting from the amendments described in subparagraph (A) is barred by any law or rule of law, such credit or refund shall nevertheless be made if claim therefor is made before the date 6 months after such date of enactment.

## Charitable Deduction for Gifts of Copyright Art Works

(Section 423)

(a) ESTATE TAX.—Subsection (e) of section 2055 (relating to disallowance of deduction in certain cases) is amended by adding at the end thereof the following new paragraph:

"(4) WORKS OF ART AND THEIR COPYRIGHTS TREATED AS SEPARATE PROPERTIES IN CERTAIN CASES.—

"(A) IN GENERAL.—In the case of a qualified contribution of a work of art, the work of art and the copyright on such work of art shall be treated as separate properties for purposes of paragraph (2).

"(B) WORK OF ART DEFINED.—For purposes of this paragraph, the term 'work of art' means any tangible personal property with respect to which there is a copyright under Federal law.

"(C) QUALIFIED CONTRIBUTION DEFINED.—For purposes of this paragraph, the term 'qualified contribution' means any transfer of property to a qualified organization if the use of the property by the organization is related to the purpose or function constituting the basis for its exemption under section 501.

"(D) QUALIFIED ORGANIZATION DEFINED.—For purposes of this paragraph, the term 'qualified organization' means any organization described in section 501(c)(3) other than a private foundation (as defined in section 509). For purposes of the preceding sentence, a private operating foundation (as defined in section 4942(j)(3)) shall not be treated as a private foundation."

(b) GIFT TAX.—Subsection (c) of section 2522 is amended by adding at the end thereof the following new paragraph:

"(3) Rules similar to the rules of section 2055(e)(4) shall apply for purposes of paragraph (2)."

(c) EFFECTIVE DATES.—

(1) SUBSECTION (a).—The amendment made by subsection (a) shall apply to the estates of decedents dying after December 31, 1981.

(2) SUBSECTION (b).—The amendment made by subsection (b) shall apply to transfers after December 31, 1981.

## Gifts Made Within Three Years of Decedent's Death

(Section 424)

(a) GENERAL RULE.—Section 2035 (relating to adjustments for gifts made within 3 years of decedent's death) is amended by adding at the end thereof the following new subsection:

"(d) DECEDENTS DYING AFTER 1981.—

"(1) IN GENERAL.—Except as otherwise provided in this subsection, subsection (a) shall not apply to the estate of a decedent dying after December 31, 1981.

"(2) EXCEPTIONS FOR CERTAIN TRANSFERS.—Paragraph (1) shall not apply to a transfer of an interest in property which is included in the value of the gross estate under section 2036, 2037, 2038, 2041, or 2042 or would have been included under any of such sections if such interest had been retained by the decedent.

"(3) 3-YEAR RULE RETAINED FOR CERTAIN PURPOSES.—Paragraph (1) shall not apply for purposes of—

"(A) section 303(b) (relating to distributions in redemption of stock to pay death taxes),

"(B) section 2032A (relating to special valuation of certain farm, etc., real property),

"(C) section 6166 (relating to extension of time for payment of estate tax where estate consists largely of interest in closely held business), and

"(D) subchapter C of chapter 64 (relating to lien for taxes)."

(b) EFFECTIVE DATE.—The amendment made by subsection (a) shall apply to the estates of decedents dying after December 31, 1981.

## Postponement of Generation-Skipping Tax Effective Date

(Section 428)

Section 2006(c) of the Tax Reform Act of 1976 (relating to the effective dates of generation-skipping provisions), as amended by section 702(n)(1) of the Revenue Act of 1978 is amended by striking out "January 1, 1982" in paragraph (2)(B) of such section and inserting in lieu thereof "January 1, 1983".

## Estate Tax Credit for Transfer to Smithsonian

(Section 429)

Upon transfer to the Smithsonian Institution, within thirty days following the date of the enactment of this Act, of all right, title, and interests held by the Dorothy Meserve Kunhardt trust and the estate of Dorothy Meserve Kunhardt in the collection of approximately seven thousand two hundred and fifty Mathew Brady glass plate negatives and the Alexander Gardner imperial portrait print of Abraham Lincoln, there shall be allowed as a credit, effective as of the date upon which the return was due to be filed, against the tax imposed by section 2001 (relating to the imposition of estate tax) on such estate an amount equal to the lesser of—

(1) such tax,

(2) the fair market value of such negatives and such print, or

(3) $700,000.

## Increases in Annual Gift Tax Exclusion

(Section 441)

(a) INCREASE IN ANNUAL EXCLUSION.—Subsection (b) of section 2503 (relating to annual gift tax exclusion) is amended by striking out "$3,000" and inserting in lieu thereof "$10,000".

(b) UNLIMITED EXCLUSION FOR CERTAIN TRANSFERS.—Section 2503 (defining taxable gifts) is amended by adding at the end thereof the following new subsection:

"(e) EXCLUSION FOR CERTAIN TRANSFERS FOR EDUCATIONAL EXPENSES OR MEDICAL EXPENSES.—

"(1) IN GENERAL.—Any qualified transfer shall not be treated as a transfer of property by gift for purposes of this chapter.

"(2) QUALIFIED TRANSFER.—For purposes of this subsection, the term 'qualified transfer' means any amount paid on behalf of an individual—

"(A) as tuition to an educational organization described in section 170(b)(1)(A)(ii) for the education or training of such individual, or

"(B) to any person who provides medical care (as defined in section 213(e)) with respect to such individual as payment for such medical care."

(c) EFFECTIVE DATES.—

(1) IN GENERAL.—Except as provided in paragraph (2), the amendments made by this section shall apply to transfers after December 31, 1981.

(2) TRANSITIONAL RULE.—If—

(A) an instrument executed before the date which is 30 days after the date of the enactment of this Act provides for a power of appointment which may be exercised during any period after December 31, 1981,

(B) such power of appointment is expressly defined in

terms of, or by reference to, the amount of the gift tax exclusion under section 2503(b) of the Internal Revenue Code of 1954 (or the corresponding provision of prior law),

(C) the instrument described in subparagraph (A) has not been amended on or after the date which is 30 days after the date of the enactment of this Act, and

(D) the State has not enacted a statute applicable to such gift under which such power of appointment is to be construed as being defined in terms of, or by reference to, the amount of the exclusion under such section 2503(b) after its amendment by subsection (a),

then the amendment made by subsection (a) shall not apply to such gift.

## Time for Payment of Gift Taxes

(Section 442)

(a) AMENDMENTS TO SUBCHAPTER A OF CHAPTER 12.—

(1) SECTION 2501.—Subsection (a) of section 2501 (relating to imposition of gift tax) is amended by striking out "calendar quarter" each place it appears and inserting in lieu thereof "calendar year".

(2) SECTION 2502.—Section 2502 (relating to rate of tax) is amended to read as follows:

"SEC. 2502. RATE OF TAX.

"(a) COMPUTATION OF TAX.—The tax imposed by section 2501 for each calendar year shall be an amount equal to the excess of—

"(1) a tentative tax, computed in accordance with the rate schedule set forth in section 2001(c), on the aggregate sum of the taxable gifts for such calendar year and for each of the preceding calendar periods, over

"(2) a tentative tax, computed in accordance with such rate schedule, on the aggregate sum of the taxable gifts for each of the preceding calendar periods.

"(b) PRECEDING CALENDAR PERIOD.—Whenever used in this title in connection with the gift tax imposed by this chapter, the term 'preceding calendar period' means—

"(1) calendar years 1932 and 1970 and all calendar years intervening between calendar year 1932 and calendar year 1970,

"(2) the first calendar quarter of calendar year 1971 and all calendar quarters intervening between such calendar quarter and the first calendar quarter of calendar year 1982, and

"(3) all calendar years after 1981 and before the calendar year for which the tax is being computed.

For purposes of paragraph (1), the term 'calendar year 1932' includes only that portion of such year after June 6, 1932.

"(c) TAX TO BE PAID BY DONOR.—The tax imposed by section 2501 shall be paid by the donor."

(3) SECTION 2503.—

(A) Subsection (a) of section 2503 is amended to read as follows:

"(a) GENERAL DEFINITION.—The term 'taxable gifts' means the total amount of gifts made during the calendar year, less the deductions provided in subchapter C (section 2522 and following)."

(B) The first sentence of subsection (b) of section 2503 is amended to read as follows: "In the case of gifts (other than gifts of future interests in property) made to any person by the donor during the calendar year, the first $10,000 of such gifts to such person shall not, for purposes of subsection (a), be included in the total amount of gifts made during such year."

(4) SECTION 2504.—

(A) Subsection (a) of section 2504 is amended to read as follows:

"(a) IN GENERAL.—In computing taxable gifts for preceding calendar periods for purposes of computing the tax for any calendar year—

"(1) there shall be treated as gifts such transfers as were considered to be gifts under the gift tax laws applicable to the calendar period in which the transfers were made,

"(2) there shall be allowed such deductions as were provided for under such laws, and

"(3) the specific exemption in the amount (if any) allowable under section 2521 (as in effect before its repeal by the Tax Reform Act of 1976) shall be applied in all computations in respect of preceding calendar periods ending before January 1, 1977, for purposes of computing the tax for any calendar year."

(B) Subsection (b) of section 2504 is amended—

(i) by striking out "preceding calendar years and calendar quarters" and inserting in lieu thereof "preceding calendar periods",

(ii) by striking out "the years and calendar quarters" and inserting in lieu thereof "the periods",

(iii) by striking out "such years and calendar quarters" and inserting in lieu thereof "such preceding calendar periods", and

(iv) by striking out "PRECEDING YEARS AND QUARTERS" in the subsection heading and inserting in lieu thereof "PRECEDING CALENDAR PERIODS".

(C) Subsection (c) of section 2504 is amended—

(i) by striking out "preceding calendar year or calendar quarter" each place it appears and inserting in lieu thereof "preceding calendar period",

(ii) by striking out "under this chapter for any calendar quarter" and inserting in lieu thereof "under this chapter for any calendar year",

(iii) by striking out "section 2502(c)" and inserting in lieu thereof "section 2502(b)", and

(iv) by striking out "PRECEDING CALENDAR YEARS AND QUARTERS" in the subsection heading and inserting in lieu thereof "PRECEDING CALENDAR PERIODS".

(D) The section heading for section 2504 is amended by striking out "PRECEDING YEARS AND QUARTERS" and inserting in lieu thereof "PRECEDING CALENDAR PERIODS".

(E) The table of sections for subchapter A of chapter 12 is amended by striking out "preceding years and quarters" in the item relating to section 2504 and inserting in lieu thereof "preceding calendar periods".

(5) SECTION 2505.—

(A) Subsection (a) of section 2505 is amended—

(i) by striking out "each calendar quarter" and inserting in lieu thereof "each calendar year", and

(ii) by striking out "preceding calendar quarters" and inserting in lieu thereof "preceding calendar periods".

(B) Subsection (d) of section 2505 is amended by striking out "calendar quarter" each place it appears and inserting in lieu thereof "calendar year".

(b) AMENDMENTS TO SUBCHAPTER B OF CHAPTER 12.—

(1) SECTION 2512.—Subsection (b) of section 2512 is amended by striking out "calendar quarter" and inserting in lieu thereof "calendar year".

(2) SECTION 2513.—

(A) Section 2513(a) is amended by striking out "calendar quarter" each place it appears and inserting in lieu thereof "calendar year".

(B) Paragraph (2) of section 2513(b) is amended by striking out "calendar quarter" in the matter preceding subparagraph (A) and inserting in lieu thereof "calendar year".

(C) Subparagraph (A) of subsection (b)(2) of section 2513 is amended to read as follows:

"(A) The consent may not be signified after the 15th day of April following the close of such year, unless before such 15th day no return has been filed for such year by either spouse, in which case the consent may not be signified after a return for such year is filed by either spouse."

(D) Subparagraph (B) of subsection (b)(2) of section 2513 is amended—

(i) by striking out "the consent" and inserting in lieu thereof "The consent", and

(ii) by striking out "such calendar quarter" and inserting in lieu thereof "such year".

(E) Subsection (c) of section 2513 is amended—

(i) by striking out "calendar quarter" and inserting in lieu thereof "calendar year", and

(ii) by striking out "15th day of the second month following the close of such quarter" and inserting in lieu "15th day of April following the close of such year".

(F) Subsection (d) of section 2513 is amended—

(i) by striking out "any calendar quarter" and inserting in lieu thereof "any calendar year", and

(ii) by striking out "such calendar quarter" and inserting in lieu thereof "such year".

(c) AMENDMENT TO SUBCHAPTER C OF CHAPTER 12.—Section 2522 is amended by striking out "quarter" each place it appears and inserting in lieu thereof "year".

(d) MISCELLANEOUS AMENDMENTS.—

(1) Paragraph (2) of subsection (d) of section 1015 (relating to increased basis for gift tax paid) is amended—

(A) by striking out "calendar quarter (or calendar year if the gift was made before January 1, 1971)" and inserting in lieu thereof "calendar year (or preceding calendar period)", and

(B) by striking out "calendar quarter or year" each place it appears and inserting in lieu thereof "calendar year or period".

(2) Section 6019 (relating to gift tax returns) is amended by striking out subsection (b).

(3) Subsection (b) of section 6075 (relating to time for filing gift tax returns) is amended to read as follows:

"(b) GIFT TAX RETURNS.—

"(1) GENERAL RULE.—Returns made under section 6019 (relating to gift taxes) shall be filed on or before the 15th day of April following the close of the calendar year.

"(2) EXTENSION WHERE TAXPAYER GRANTED EXTENSION FOR FILING INCOME TAX RETURN.—Any extension of time granted the taxpayer for filing the return of income taxes imposed by subtitle A for any taxable year which is a calendar year shall be deemed to be also an extension of time granted the taxpayer for filing the return under section 6019 for such calendar year.

"(3) COORDINATION WITH DUE DATE FOR ESTATE TAX RETURN.— Notwithstanding paragraphs (1) and (2), the time for filing the return made under section 6019 for the calendar year which includes the date of death of the donor shall not be later than the time (including extensions) for filing the return made under section 6018 (relating to estate tax returns) with respect to such donor."

(4) Paragraph (1) of section 6212(c) (relating to notice of deficiency) is amended by striking out "calendar quarter" and inserting in lieu thereof "calendar year".

(e) EFFECTIVE DATE.—The amendments made by this section shall apply with respect to gifts made after December 31, 1981.

## Windfall Profit Tax Exemption for Child Care Agencies

(Section 604)

(a) EXEMPTION OF CHILD CARE AGENCIES FROM TAX.—Subparagraph (A) of section 4994(b)(1) (relating to charitable interests exempt from windfall profit tax) is amended by redesignating clause (ii) as clause (iii) and by adding after clause (i) the following new clause:

"(ii) held by an organization described in section 170(c)(2) which is organized and operated primarily for the residential placement, care, or treatment of delinquent, dependent, orphaned, neglected, or handicapped children, or".

(b) PERIOD INTEREST REQUIRED TO BE HELD.—

(1) IN GENERAL.—Subparagraph (B) of section 4994(b)(1) is amended to read as follows:

"(B) such interest was held on January 21, 1980, and at all times thereafter before the last day of the taxable period, by the organization described in clause (i) or (ii) of subparagraph (A), or subclause (I) of subparagraph (A)(iii)."

(2) INTERESTS HELD FOR THE BENEFIT OF CHILD CARE AGENCIES.— Paragraph (2) of section 4994(b) is amended—

(A) by striking out "paragraph (1)(A)(ii)" and inserting in lieu thereof "clause (ii) or (iii) of paragraph (1)(A)", and

(B) by striking out "paragraph (1)(A)(i)" each place it appears and inserting in lieu thereof "clause (i) or (ii) of paragraph (1)(A)".

(c) CONFORMING AMENDMENTS.—

(1) Clause (i) of section 4994(b)(1)(A) is amended by striking out "or" at the end thereof.

(2) Subclause (II) of section 4994(b)(1)(A)(ii) is amended by inserting "or (ii)" after "clause (i)".

(d) EFFECTIVE DATE.—The amendments made by this section shall apply to taxable periods beginning after December 31, 1980.

## Tax Penalty for Valuation Overstatements

(Section 722)

(a) VALUATION OVERSTATEMENTS.—

(1) In GENERAL.—Subchapter A of chapter 68 (relating to additions to tax) is amended by redesignating section 6659 as section 6660 and by inserting after section 6658 the following new section:

"SEC. 6659. ADDITION TO TAX IN THE CASE OF VALUATION OVERSTATE-MENTS FOR PURPOSES OF THE INCOME TAX.

"(a) ADDITION TO THE TAX.—If—
    "(1) an individual, or
    "(2) a closely held corporation or a personal service corporation,
has an underpayment of the tax imposed by chapter 1 for the taxable year which is attributable to a valuation overstatement, then there shall be added to the tax an amount equal to the applicable percentage of the underpayment so attributable.

"(b) APPLICABLE PERCENTAGE DEFINED.—For purposes of subsection (a), the applicable percentage shall be determined under the following table:

| "If the valuation claimed is the following percent of the correct valuation— | The applicable percentage is: |
|---|---|
| 150 percent or more but not more than 200 percent | 10 |
| More than 200 percent but not more than 250 percent | 20 |
| More than 250 percent | 30 |

"(c) VALUATION OVERSTATEMENT DEFINED.—
    "(1) In GENERAL.—For purposes of this section, there is a valuation overstatement if the value of any property, or the adjusted basis of any property, claimed on any return exceeds 150 percent of the amount determined to be the correct amount of such valuation or adjusted basis (as the case may be).
    "(2) PROPERTY MUST HAVE BEEN ACQUIRED WITHIN LAST 5 YEARS.—This section shall not apply to any property which, as of the close of the taxable year for which there is a valuation overstatement, has been held by the taxpayer for more than 5 years.

"(d) UNDERPAYMENT MUST BE AT LEAST $1,000.—This section shall not apply if the underpayment for the taxable year attributable to the valuation overstatement is less than $1,000.

"(e) AUTHORITY TO WAIVE.—The Secretary may waive all or any part of the addition to the tax provided by this section on a showing by the taxpayer that there was a reasonable basis for the valuation or adjusted basis claimed on the return and that such claim was made in good faith.

"(f) OTHER DEFINITIONS.—For purposes of this section—
    "(1) UNDERPAYMENT.—The term 'underpayment' has the meaning given to such term by section 6653(c)(1).
    "(2) CLOSELY HELD CORPORATION.—The term 'closely held corporation' means any corporation described in section 465(a)(1)(C).
    "(3) PERSONAL SERVICE CORPORATION.—The term 'personal service corporation' means any corporation which is a service

organization (within the meaning of section 414(m)(3))."

(2) CLERICAL AMENDMENT.—The table of sections for sub-chapter A of chapter 68 is amended by striking out the last item and inserting in lieu thereof the following:

"Sec. 6659. Addition to tax in the case of valuation overstatements for purposes of the income tax.
"Sec. 6660. Applicable rules."

(3) TECHNICAL AMENDMENT.—Subsection (c) of section 5684 (relating to penalties for the payment and collection of liquor taxes) and subsection (d) of section 5761 (relating to civil penalties) are each amended by striking out "6659" in the heading and text thereof and inserting in lieu thereof "6660"

(4) EFFECTIVE DATE.—The amendments made by this subsection shall apply to returns filed after December 31, 1981.


## Private Foundation Distribution Requirements

(Section 823)

(a) GENERAL RULE.—
(1) Paragraph (1) of section 4942(d) (defining distributable amount) is amended by striking "or the adjusted net income (whichever is higher)".

(2) Paragraph (3)(A) of section 4942(j) (defining operating foundation) is amended to read as follows:
"(A) which makes qualifying distributions (within the meaning of paragraph (1) or (2) of subsection (g)) directly for the active conduct of the activities constituting the purpose or function for which it is organized and operated equal to substantially all of the lesser of—
"(i) its adjusted net income (as defined in subsection (f)), and
"(ii) its minimum investment return; and".

(3) Paragraph (3) of section 4942(j) is amended by adding at the end thereof the following new sentence: "Notwithstanding the provisons of subparagraph (A), if the qualifying distributions (within the meaning of paragraph (1) or (2) of subsection (g)) of an organization for the taxable year exceed the minimum investment return for the taxable year, clause (ii) of subparagraph (A) shall not apply unless substantially all of such qualifying distributions are made directly for the active conduct of the activities constituting the purpose or function for which it is organized and operated."
(b) EFFECTIVE DATE.—The amendments made by this section shall apply to taxable years beginning after December 31, 1981.

## Extension of Prohibition on Fringe Benefit Regulations

(Section 801)

Section 1 of the Act entitled "An Act to prohibit the issuance of regulations on the taxation of fringe benefits, and for other purposes", approved October 7, 1978 (Public Law 95-427), is amended by striking out "May 31, 1981" each place it appears and inserting in lieu thereof "December 31, 1983".

## Extension of Prepaid Legal Services Exclusion

(Section 802)

(a) EXTENSION.—Section 120 (relating to amounts received under qualified group legal services plans) is amended by adding at the end thereof the following new subsection:

"(e) TERMINATION.—This section shall not apply to taxable years ending after December 31, 1984."

(b) CONFORMING AMENDMENT.—Paragraph (1) of section 2134(e) of the Tax Reform Act of 1976 (relating to effective date) is amended by striking out ", and ending before January 1, 1982".

# Estimated Revenue Effects of the Economic Recovery Tax Act of 1981

Table 1.—SUMMARY OF ESTIMATED REVENUE EFFECTS OF THE PROVISIONS OF H.R. 4242 AS APPROVED BY THE CONFERENCE COMMITTEE, FISCAL YEARS 1981–86

[In millions of dollars]

| Provision | 1981 | 1982 | 1983 | 1984 | 1985 | 1986 |
|---|---|---|---|---|---|---|
| Individual income tax provisions | −39 | −26,929 | −71,098 | −114,684 | −148,237 | −196,143 |
| Business tax cut provisions | −1,562 | −10,657 | −18,599 | −28,275 | −39,269 | −54,468 |
| Energy tax provisions | | −1,320 | −1,742 | −2,242 | −2,837 | −3,619 |
| Savings incentive provisions | | −263 | −1,821 | −4,215 | −5,740 | −8,375 |
| Estate and gift tax provisions | | −204 | −2,114 | −3,218 | −4,248 | −5,568 |
| Tax straddles provisions [1] | 37 | 623 | 327 | 273 | 249 | 229 |
| Administrative provisions | | 1,182 | 2,048 | 1,856 | 718 | 592 |
| Miscellaneous provisions | −1 | −88 | 267 | 561 | 61 | −275 |
| Total Revenue Effect | −1,565 | −37,656 | −92,732 | −149,944 | −199,303 | −267,627 |

[1] See footnote 9 for table 2.

Table 2.—ESTIMATED REVENUE EFFECTS OF THE PROVISIONS OF H.R. 4242 AS APPROVED BY THE CONFERENCE COMMITTEE, FISCAL YEARS 1981–86

[In millions of dollars]

| Provision | 1981 | 1982 | 1983 | 1984 | 1985 | 1986 |
|---|---|---|---|---|---|---|
| **Individual income tax provisions:** | | | | | | |
| Rate cuts [1] | | −25,793 | −65,703 | −104,512 | −122,652 | −143,832 |
| 20 percent rate on capital gains for portion of 1981 | −39 | −355 | | | | |
| Deduction for two-earner married couples | | −419 | −4,418 | −9,090 | −10,973 | −12,624 |
| Indexing | | | | | −12,941 | −35,848 |
| Child and dependent care credit | | −19 | −191 | −237 | −296 | −356 |
| Charitable contributions deduction for nonitemizers | | −26 | −189 | −219 | −681 | −2,696 |
| Rollover period for sale of residence | ([3]) | ([4]) | ([4]) | ([4]) | ([4]) | ([4]) |
| Increased exclusion on sale of residence | ([3]) | −18 | −53 | −63 | −76 | −91 |
| Changes in taxation of foreign earned income | | −299 | −544 | −563 | −618 | −696 |
| Total, individual tax reductions | −39 | −26,929 | −71,098 | −114,684 | −148,237 | −196,143 |
| **Business tax cut provisions:** | | | | | | |
| Capital cost recovery provisions | −1,503 | −9,569 | −16,796 | −26,250 | −37,285 | −52,797 |
| Corporate rate reductions | | −116 | −365 | −521 | −565 | −610 |
| Credit for rehabilitation expenditures | −9 | −129 | −208 | −239 | −302 | −409 |
| Credit for used property | −24 | −61 | −74 | −85 | −137 | −198 |
| Credit for increasing research activities | | −448 | −708 | −858 | −847 | −485 |
| Permit complete allocation to domestic deductions of all domestically performed R&D | | −57 | −120 | −62 | ([2]) | |
| Charitable contributions of scientific property used for research | ([2]) | ([2]) | ([2]) | ([2]) | ([2]) | ([2]) |
| Increase in accumulated earnings credit | | ([2]) | −33 | −36 | −40 | −44 |
| Subchapter S shareholders | | ([2]) | ([2]) | ([2]) | ([2]) | ([2]) |
| LIFO inventories and small business accounting | | −68 | −184 | −192 | −145 | −64 |
| Reorganizations of certain savings and loan associations [5] | ([2]) | ([2]) | ([2]) | ([2]) | ([2]) | ([2]) |
| Commercial bank bad debt deduction | | −15 | −15 | | | |
| Conversion of mutual savings banks | −5 | −10 | −12 | −18 | −22 | −25 |
| Extension and modification of targeted jobs tax credit | | −63 | −13 | 57 | 117 | 161 |
| Incentive stock options | ([2]) | ([2]) | ([2]) | ([2]) | 11 | 21 |
| Motor carrier operating rights [6] | −21 | −121 | −71 | −71 | −54 | −18 |
| Total, business tax cut provisions | −1,562 | −10,657 | −18,599 | −28,275 | −39,269 | −54,468 |
| **Energy provisions:** | | | | | | |
| $2,500 royalty credit for 1981; exemption for 1982 and thereafter | | −1,220 | −947 | −986 | −1,193 | −1,279 |
| Reduction in tax of newly discovered oil | | −75 | −255 | −520 | −867 | −1,528 |
| Exempt independent producer stripper well oil | | | −525 | −721 | −762 | −797 |
| Exemption from windfall profit tax for child care agencies | | −25 | −15 | −15 | −15 | −15 |
| Total, energy provisions | | −1,320 | −1,742 | −2,242 | −2,837 | −3,619 |

Table 2.—ESTIMATED REVENUE EFFECTS OF THE PROVISIONS OF H.R. 4242 AS APPROVED BY THE CONFERENCE COMMITTEE, FISCAL YEARS 1981-86—Continued

[In millions of dollars]

| Provision | 1981 | 1982 | 1983 | 1984 | 1985 | 1986 |
|---|---|---|---|---|---|---|
| Savings incentives provisions: [7] | | | | | | |
| Individual retirement savings | | −229 | −1,339 | −1,849 | −2,325 | −2,582 |
| Self-employed plans | | −56 | −157 | −173 | −183 | −201 |
| Exclusion of interest on certain savings certificates | | −398 | −1,791 | −1,142 | | |
| 15 percent net interest exclusion | | | | | −1,124 | −3,126 |
| Repeal of $200 exclusion of interest and return to prior law $100 dividend exclusion | | 566 | 1,916 | | | |
| Reinvestment of dividends in public utility stock | | −130 | −365 | −416 | −449 | −278 |
| Employee stock ownership plans | | (2) | −61 | −628 | −1,659 | −2,188 |
| Group legal service plans | | −16 | −24 | −7 | | |
| Total, savings incentives provisions | | −263 | −1,821 | −4,215 | −5,740 | −8,375 |
| Estate and gift tax provisions: | | | | | | |
| Increase in unified credit | | (2) | −1,077 | −1,981 | −2,811 | −3,834 |
| Reduction in maximum rates of tax | | (2) | −172 | −371 | −556 | −890 |
| Unlimited marital deduction | | (2) | 303 | −304 | −311 | −300 |
| Current use of certain farm etc., real property | | −18 | −280 | −295 | −326 | −319 |
| Extensions of time for payment of estate tax | | (2) | −20 | −16 | −15 | −12 |
| Tax treatment of contributions of works of art, etc. | | (2) | (2) | (2) | (2) | (2) |
| Transfers of gifts with 3 years of death | | (2) | −58 | −50 | −42 | −38 |
| Repeal of deduction for bequests to minor children | | (8) | (8) | (8) | (8) | (8) |
| Increase in annual gift tax exclusion | | −123 | −204 | −201 | −187 | −175 |
| Annual filing and payment of gifts taxes | | −63 | (2) | (2) | (2) | (2) |
| Total, estate and gift tax provisions | | −204 | −2,114 | −3,218 | −4,248 | −5,568 |
| Tax straddles [9] | 37 | 623 | 327 | 273 | 249 | 229 |
| Administrative provisions: | | | | | | |
| Changes in interest rate for overpayments and underpayments | | 100 | (2) | 100 | −100 | 60 |
| Changes in certain penalties | (8) | (8) | (8) | (8) | (8) | (8) |
| Cash management—changes in estimated tax payment requirements for large corporations | | 614 | 1,522 | 1,190 | 201 | −142 |
| Individual threshold for filing estimated payments increased to $500 | | −44 | −29 | −38 | −40 | −38 |
| Financing of railroad retirement system | | 512 | 555 | 604 | 657 | 712 |
| Total, administrative provisions | | 1,182 | 2,048 | 1,856 | 718 | 592 |

Table 2.—ESTIMATED REVENUE EFFECTS OF THE PROVISIONS OF H.R. 4242 AS APPROVED BY THE CONFERENCE COMMITTEE, FISCAL YEARS 1981–86—Continued

[In millions of dollars]

| Provision | 1981 | 1982 | 1983 | 1984 | 1985 | 1986 |
|---|---|---|---|---|---|---|
| Miscellaneous provisions: | | | | | | |
| State legislators travel expenses | | −9 | −5 | −6 | −6 | −7 |
| Taxation of investment income of campaign funds | (2) | (2) | (2) | (2) | (2) | (2) |
| Tax-exempt bonds for volunteer fire departments | | (10) | (10) | (10) | (10) | (10) |
| Charitable contributions by corporations | | −44 | −93 | −102 | −112 | −123 |
| Unemployment tax status of fishing boat services | | (10) | | | | |
| Excise tax on telephone service | | | 435 | 766 | 309 | |
| Amortization of construction period interest and taxes | | −14 | −33 | −27 | −23 | −21 |
| Amortization of low-income housing rehabilitation expenditures | −1 | −8 | −16 | −25 | −35 | −39 |
| Foreign investment in U.S. real property | (2) | (2) | (2) | (2) | (2) | (2) |
| Payout requirements of private foundations | (2) | (2) | (2) | (2) | (2) | (2) |
| Imputed interest rates on installment sales | (2) | (2) | (2) | (2) | (2) | (2) |
| Deduction for gifts and awards | | −4 | −5 | −6 | −7 | −9 |
| Industrial development bonds for mass transit | | (10) | −7 | −29 | −54 | −64 |
| Deduction for certain adoption expenses | | −9 | −9 | −10 | −11 | −12 |
| Total, miscellaneous provisions | −1 | −88 | 267 | 561 | 61 | −275 |
| Grand total all provisions | −1,565 | −37,656 | −92,732 | −149,944 | −199,303 | −267,627 |

[1] These figures include the increase in outlays attribute to the earned income credit which results from reduction in tax rates. These outlays are: $4 million in fiscal year 1982, $31 million in 1983, $44 million in 1984, $41 million in 1985, and $38 million in 1986.
[2] Loss of less than $5 million.
[3] Negligible.
[4] Loss of less than $10 million.
[5] This estimate is based on limited information about reorganizations that were planned even without this provision. If such reorganizations would have increased markedly without this provision, the revenue loss could be substantial.
[6] Includes a portion of the $36 million in tax liabilities for calendar year 1980.
[7] These estimates were made using the rate schedule proposed by the bill. This approach results in a lower revenue loss than one that would have been obtained if the present law rates had been used.
[8] Gain of less than $5 million.
[9] Revenue effects do not reflect transactions entered into after December 31, 1981. Total revenue effects of subsequent years might be affected by judicial decisions interpreting present law.
[10] Loss of less than $1 million.

166